GHOUL
BRITANNIA

GHOUL BRITANNIA

BRITANNIA

Notes from a Haunted Isle

ANDREW MARTIN

First published in 2009 by

Short Books

3A Exmouth House

Pine Street

EC1R 0JH

10 9 8 7 6 5 4 3 2 1

A CIP catalogue record for this book
is available from the British Library.

ISBN 978-1-906021-85-6

Cover design and illustrations © Nathan Burton

Printed in Great Britain by Clays, Suffolk

CONTENTS

INTRODUCTION
The Moon Still Rises –
or *British Ghostliness Today*

On the face of it, British ghostliness is a thing of the past. It would seem to be another of those things that we pioneered and did well, but have now given up on, like making motorbikes or running decent pubs.

Ghosts weren't quite uniquely ours, but in his introduction to *Phantom Britain*, published in 1975 with the nifty subtitle, 'This Spectre'd Isle', Marcus Alexander wrote, 'In Italy, a frequent beginning to a ghost story is, *C'era una volta un castello in Cornovaglia*...: There was once a castle in Cornwall...'

In his *A-Z of British Ghosts* (1994), Peter Underwood, author and ghost hunter, mentions that Brede Place, near Rye in Sussex, was described by the architect Sir Edwin Lutyens as 'the most interesting haunted house in Sussex.' The most haunted town or city in Britain is sometimes said to be my birthplace, York. According to *The York Book* (2003), it has a reputation as 'the most haunted city in

Europe, with a rumoured 140 ghosts', but it isn't even mentioned in Christina Hole's book, *Haunted England* (1940), which is no criticism of her, but just shows the embarrassment of riches available to the British supernaturalist.

There does seem to be general agreement that Pluckley in Kent is the most haunted village in Britain. Pluckley is on the route of a phantom coach and horses; there's an old mill haunted by an old miller, a ghostly monk, a Red Lady, a White Lady, a poltergeist in The Black Horse Inn, over the road from which the ghost of a schoolmaster who hanged himself has been seen dangling from a tree, and so on. Pluckley is like Fairfield, 'a little village lying near the Portsmouth Road about halfway between London and the sea' in the frequently anthologised short story, 'The Ghost Ship' by Richard Middleton. Fairfield is entirely populated by ghosts, and so this is an amusing ghost story – which becomes less amusing when you know that its impoverished author committed suicide with chloroform in Brussels in 1911, leaving a note announcing that he was 'going adventuring again'.

I daresay that any book on the Pluckley ghosts would have a respectable sale, especially in Pluckley. Research conducted by Theos, the theology think-tank, found that four in ten Britons believe in ghosts, and any bookshop, however small, will have a supernatural section just as it will have a gardening section. The law of averages dictated that, when Google photographed the entire country for its 'Street View' project, it would capture a ghost minding its own business. This occurred in Tiger Bay, Cardiff. the *Sun* reported, 'The footage appears to show a woman dressed in a long skirt, crisp blouse, bow tie, blue boater hat and scarf shimmering above the pavement.'

The profession of medium has not entirely died. Derek Acorah, 'Britain's Number One medium' (that's more or less official, apparently), makes a very good living indeed, and we will see him at work later. But I suspect that most of us regard the whole business of contacting the dead as rather old hat; a hobby of yesteryear, like hopscotch or going to the beach with a metal detector.

Oh, the curtain still rises every night, which is to say that the darkness falls over Britain and the moon rises, but the lighting is not what it was, for a start. The candles and oil lamps, which were capable of producing such moody and subtle effects, have been replaced by crude electric light. The old props manager has retired, taking with him his stock of velvet curtains so handy for half-concealing all manner of things; his French windows, primed to spring open without warning; his stock of grandfather clocks with especially ominous ticks. Admittedly, the sound man lingers on. He can still drum up some rustling leaves on autumnal trees, or trains that whistle (after a fashion), but there's a certain loss of tone even here.

And you can't get the *staff*...

There are no wall-eyed yokels who, when asked whether the black dog or white lady is due to walk on a particular evening, can be relied on to reply, 'Thuy do zay zo.' There are insufficient spurned aristocratic beauties, or naïve young Oxbridge men keen to inhabit abandoned mansions: 'an ideal spot for some quiet study'. There are very few occultists in smoking jackets for whom Latin is practically a first language. I've also noticed a shortage of proper *rectors*. Instead we have depressingly hearty-sounding 'team rectors', and I bet they don't live in rectories.

According to the literary critics, the moment of the ghost story has passed. That moment began in the mid-nineteenth century, when people stopped believing in ghosts sufficiently to find them entertaining; or at any rate when Charles Darwin seemed to leave no room at all for anything spiritual or mysterious. This was – and is – an airless, claustrophobic feeling, and it prompted among the middle class the rise of Spiritualism (of which more later) and of séances, held in low-lit drawing rooms either just before or just after dinner, depending on how long contacting the dead was thought likely to take.

For a while, The Great War boosted Spiritualism, there being so many more dead to contact, but the ghost story was one of the war's early casualties. Headless horsemen could not be so lightly invoked after a fair percentage of the country's young men had had their heads blown off. Ghost story writers lost their confidence, and their tales either became more gory in an attempt to keep up, or self-deprecatingly comic. Julia Briggs, in *Night Visitors: The Rise and Fall of the English Ghost Story* (1977), argues that the rise of Freudianism had also made authors who might have written ghost stories too wary of being analysed to do so.

As a result, the genre began to die, which makes those of us who refuse to give up on ghostliness feel self-conscious about our interest.

For example...

I was sitting in a traffic jam on the North Circular recently or – to put the matter in an even more unghostly way – on the A406 just by the turn-off to Brent Cross. It was the middle of a sunny day, and I was listening to some Victorian ghost stories on CD, a fact that became embarrassingly public as the traffic seized up, since the volume was loud and the windows were down. In the next lane a kid of about twenty sat in a 'pimped up' Mini. The particular story playing was 'Narrative of the Ghost of a Hand' by Sheridan Le Fanu, read by Richard Pasco. As Le Fanu/Pasco boomed from my car window: 'The annoyances described did not begin till the end of August, when, one evening, Mrs Prosser, quite alone...' the kid looked at me in disgust. He obviously thought I was... well, what? Behind the times? Morbid?

But would he happily walk through a remote forest at midnight? I doubt he would, and not for fear of physical attack, but for fear of something else. My wife certainly wouldn't. It's not so much that she's scared of ghosts as that she refuses to have anything at all to do with them. They are too proximate to the subject of death. My younger son has the same approach. If I leave one of my collections of ghost stories in his bedroom in the early evening, he will climb out of bed, and return them to me, saying tartly, 'These are yours, I think.' I admit that I once tested him out by deliberately leaving ghost stories in his room, and the swiftness with which they were returned suggested to me that, before going to sleep, he checks his room to make sure there are no ghost stories in it.

Ghostliness has a power over us individually, and perhaps it will soon regain its power over us as a society. A friend of mine, a legal academic called Tatiana, is a connoisseur of ghost stories. She argues that an interest in ghosts arises 'when there's a disjunction between one paradigm and another'. We in Britain are certainly still suffering the after-shock of the Victorian crisis of faith, but the plates are also shifting beneath our own society. I'm thinking of the loss of economic confidence; the apocalyptic message of the environmentalists. And, as I will argue in my conclusion, there are other reasons more particular to Britain and its faltering sense of national identity that might dictate a reawakening of interest in our national ghosts – or at least in the ghosts of our ghosts.

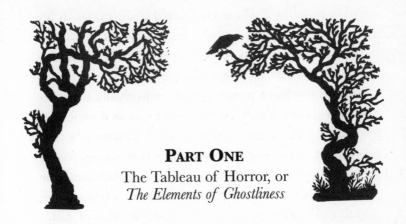

PART ONE
The Tableau of Horror, or
The Elements of Ghostliness

The group of friends with whom I discuss ghostliness is quite select, and anyone moving into our orbit is expected to respond interestingly to the question. 'Have you ever seen a ghost?' Short of an actual sighting, some account of ghostliness will do. I hope the meaning of that word will become clear in the course of this book, incidentally. You could say it was the desperate, vertiginous feeling that death is definitely going to happen, and that something even worse might follow. Or you might say, less melodramatically, that it's something that makes the hairs on the back of your neck stick up, a cliché that Rudyard Kipling tried to refine in 'My Own True Ghost Story' (1888): 'It is a mistake to say that hair stands up. The skin of the head tightens and you can feel a faint, prickly, bristling all over the scalp. That is the hair sitting up.' Ghostliness need not necessarily involve a death, but it always points that way.

Let's try to find a practical instance, starting with my friend Lawrence.

Lawrence is an Oxford graduate, and fluent in several languages. (Sorry about this, but ever since about 1830 it has been necessary to set out the bona fides of anyone interested in ghosts). By profession he is a radio producer who puts ghost stories onto BBC radio as often as he can. We meet by the fire in the Holly Bush pub in Hampstead, which serves appropriately Edwardian food, like oysters or Omelettes Arnold Bennett, and has the great virtue, as far as I'm concerned, of being just about the darkest pub in London. There I invite Lawrence to revisit his childhood, which gave him his taste for ghost stories, and was spent amid romantic scenery in Somerset.

He lived near Wookey Hole Caves, and would visit them regularly, listening to the cave guide's patter about the Witch of Wookey Hole. The Caves, if I might strike a prosaic note for a minute, were owned and operated as a tourist attraction by Madame Tussaud's Limited, of which Lawrence's father was a director. At an old disused paper mill near the caves, the firm kept the overspill from its London waxworks and in the mid-Seventies, Lawrence also frequented this mill: 'There was shelf after shelf of stuff, going right up into the dark rafters of the drying lofts. They had the Beatles heads in there – the early Beatles, when they were still moptops. They had Prince Charles from 1970; they had John Noakes's legs...and a guillotine, a real one from France. I mean, it had cut people's heads off.'

Lawrence's own interest is mainly in fictional ghost stories, and our sessions in the Holly Bush might begin with him returning from the bar with two pints of bitter, and starting up a conversation about some dead ghost story writer most people have never heard of: 'You know, the more I read of the works of Oliver Onions, the more worried I am about him. All his characters are so desperately isolated,' or 'Have you ever read anything by William Hope Hodgson? Interesting character: seaman, photographer, body builder...'

But Lawrence does have his very own true, albeit short, ghost story.

Lawrence's Ghost Story

It was the mid-seventies; I was about eight. It happened during the interval of an open-air amateur drama production. It was a Shakespeare, of course, and I'm pretty sure it was 'A Midsummer Night's Dream'. I walked off on my own down to the bottom of a sort of a field behind a field. It was shaded by dark trees – could have been cedars. I was looking at this pile of leaves that had been swept up together, perhaps ready for burning, when suddenly a woman sat up within it. She had dark eyes, and wore slightly old-fashioned clothes. I think of her as a 'charcoal gypsy maiden', to quote Bob Dylan. We looked at each other in total silence, probably six feet apart. It was twilight, on the verge of darkness. Looking back, it was a panic, but I felt no fear or really anything at the time. I would have been 7 or 8. I walked away back up to rejoin my family, and didn't tell anybody (in fact I don't think I thought any more about it). I didn't believe she was an actor from the play, but a 'gypsy' or 'tinker' as we charmingly called them in those days. Or, of course, she was something else.

Another ghost story friend is David. David, it is necessary for me to point out, is a photographer who has also written plays for radio and stage. He is about the best read person I know, and his portrait of The Queen (yes, *The* Queen) appeared in The National Portrait Gallery.

He has a habit, when the conversation is flagging next to the fireplace in Vat's Wine Bar in Lamb's Conduit Street, of asking, 'Have you ever seen a ghost?' Except it's not quite so brutally direct as that, but more like, 'I'm just curious... Has anyone here had an experience that might be called... well, in some way supernatural?' It generally works.

After a stuttering start, with blurted offerings such as, 'I believe in some sort of imprint, whether of past of future', or 'I've certainly had that sudden cold feeling in an old house...' or 'I've had that déjà vu thing – does that count?', someone will offer something more sustained, and in the last year, David has turned up a couple of gems, one of which is Lizzie's story, which appears at the end of this section. But often David is stuck with just me, and I give him a few of my own frissons or susceptibilities to ghostliness, while he nods politely and pretends he hasn't heard them before.

THREE OF THE AUTHOR'S OWN
SUSCEPTIBILITIES TO GHOSTLINESS:

1. If, late at night, I wake to find that my feet are sticking slightly beyond the end of the duvet, I quickly withdraw them, just in case some phenomenon that might happen to be passing by the end of my bed brushes against them, or touches them in any way. I feel that if my feet were touched I would die of shock. But sometimes I raise the stakes by deliberately thrusting my feet well beyond the end of the duvet and keeping them there, mentally challenging any such phantom, just as the protagonist in Algernon Blackwood's story, 'The Occupant of the Room' (1917), suspecting that there's something inside the locked cupboard in his hotel room, *knocks on the door.*

2. Speaking of cupboards... When I was about seven, I went to Scarborough with my parents. On a wild evening in late summer, when it was hard to distinguish between the flying rain and flying waves, I went into an amusement arcade on the South Bay. Walking up to one of the more antique machines, I read, 'See the Haunted House, 1d'. I asked my father whether he had a penny. Unfortunately, as it turned out, he did.

Before me stood not so much a haunted house as a haunted room contained in a glass case about two foot square. All the furniture was normal if antiquated, but there was a coffin in front of the fire place. I put the coin in the slot, and for quite a long time nothing happened. Then an ominous whirring began as the hundred year old mechanism grated into life.

The coffin lid opened, and a vampire sat up, but then I'd been expecting that. A curtain lifted; a white shaded spirit dropped down into the fireplace with an embarrassing clunk, and a hand came out of a box, all of which I took easily in my stride. Something about the whirring of the machine now suggested – to my mingled relief and disappointment – that it was winding down having done its worst. But just as I was about to turn around and walk away, the door of a little cupboard-in-the-wall that I hadn't noticed sprang open and a skeleton loomed forward.

That sight caused me about five years of neurosis. The trouble was that there was a very similar-looking wall cupboard at the foot of my own bed, and from then on I could not go to sleep unless the door was left ajar to exactly the right degree: not so wide open that I could see anything that might be within, but wide enough open so that anything emerging from the cupboard would not take me entirely by surprise. But no-one else (which is to say neither my father nor my mother) seemed able to take this requirement on board: they would recklessly leave the door wide open or shut it entirely.

3. And the moon bothers me. I have a waking nightmare of seeing the moon in the night sky, not two hundred and fifty thousand miles away and looking about the size of a ten pence piece, but parked close… say, two hundred miles away, so that it takes up half the sky and you can see its white, dead pock-marked face in detail.

This neurosis is of recent date, and began when I was walking along the beach at Southwold in Suffolk early on a winter's evening. It was quite dark, but I could see three illuminated ships on the horizon and, a little way beyond them, what appeared to be a great pink balloon in the process of being inflated, or a great jellyfish looming out of the sea. The ships seemed to be in conspiracy with whatever this object might be. I walked along, transfixed, and ignoring the friend's dog that I was walking (so that this dog, I later discovered, had run away). It gradually became apparent to me that this was the full moon rising out of the sea, and once it had cleared the sea it rose extremely rapidly, and with a somehow frightening sense of purpose, as though intent upon monitoring all nocturnal activity on earth.

*

David puts his own, polite gloss on these phobias of mine. For instance, he told me that Charles Dickens once played a practical joke on a carpenter by summoning him to prise open the wedged door of a cupboard in which he had placed two human skeletons.

As for the near moon, he tells me there's a Charles Addams cartoon on that theme... And I am certainly not alone in being somehow undermined by seeing things that are out of scale...

A friend of Lawrence's once had a nasty turn on catching sight of the masts and rigging of the Cutty Sark from the streets of Greenwich, and the Cutty Sark isn't so disproportionately large; nothing compared to the huge ships that used to tower over the two-up-two-down terraced houses of the London Docklands.

Somebody looking down at the ground while walking south along The Avenue in London N10 might also be disturbed to look up suddenly and see the way the central facade of Alexander Palace looms at the end of the street like a monstrous, battered version of the Victorian villas on either side.

David doesn't really have any susceptibilities of his own, so once I've told him of mine, we might talk about why we're interested in ghosts and stories of ghosts at all. To David, 'it is an intellectual game.' Ghost stories, whether fictional or real, either create a frisson or they don't. It's a no-bullshit medium. The test is pleasingly simple, and universal. As the novelist L.P. Hartley wrote: 'There is no intermediate step between success and failure. Either it comes off or it is a flop.' (And many of his were flops). The ghost story must be focused and because it comes from an oral tradition – the medieval ballad – it is usually short; terse, indeed. The narrator is often embarrassed at what he has to say. He does not 'milk' the story, but wants to make his point, and get it over with. Ghost stories in fiction or fact are – or ought to be – full of phrases like, 'I will briefly set the scene', 'There is no need to describe him further', 'There is really no more to tell.' In Victorian ghost stories especially, the haunted house is in 'B---- Street'; the man who lets it is 'Mr Y----'; the man who rents it 'Captain D----'.

For Lawrence, the ghost story is an antidote to the 'emotional incontinence' of our times. But, for all the economy of ghost stories, he finds 'wildness' in them. Each one is like an attempted gaol-break. In one of his ghost stories, M.R. James (and I am going to explain about this fellow in just a minute) has a yokel about to quote from *Hamlet* to the effect that 'There are more things in heaven and earth than are dreamt of in your philosophy', but he cuts him off because he can't bear the cliché. That line of Shakespeare's does nail it, however.

Lawrence also finds ghost stories 'relaxing', and this reminds me of what the shop assistant said when I bought the DVD of 'The Night of the Demon' (1957) – which is one of the top four British films with a supernatural theme, and concerns a psychopathic Satanist: 'It's a lovely one for when you're just recovering from flu.'

The ghost story, like the crime story, points up the listener's own relative security. Then again, the best of them do tend to revisit you at about three o'clock in the morning, like an over-rich dinner.

Lizzie's Ghost Story

[Lizzie, who is not actually called Lizzie, is an actress currently appearing in a lead role in the West End].

'It happened in Nottinghamshire in the mid-nineties. It was a house that took in theatricals – a house in the middle of a large estate, but half this house was fourteenth or fifteenth century, the other half was a new extension. It was quite cottage-y, but also quite bland: MFI furniture, wood veneer, Flotex carpet in the kitchen. The family who owned the place openly talked about the cold spots – there was one at the foot of the stairs. 'Oh, it's probably a ghost,' they'd say. They were quite proud of it. The husband had been decorating a room once, and he'd had to stop and walk out because of a strong feeling of being watched. You know, the hairs on the back of his neck had stood up. As soon as I got there I sensed something homing in on me. I'm quite sensitive to these things, and interested in them too. I might go to psychic fairs with a girlfriend for a laugh.

There were three of us from the same production staying in the house. We were appearing in a musical version of *A Christmas Carol*. I was one of Scrooge's housekeepers. He had about three in this version, whereas I don't think he has one in the novel. I seem to remember the show was written by the DJ Mike Read, so...go figure.

I was in the modern extension, which you'd think would be the least ghostly part of the house, but I was terrified every night. It was very difficult, somehow, to get to my room. As I walked along the corridor it seemed to be further and further away, like a Kafkaesque nightmare. I'd started sleeping with all the lights on, and the radio, because I knew something was coming, and one night when I was half asleep I heard a voice in my ear: 'Hello Lizzie'.

It was a little girl's voice, quite mischievous – naughty. The next day I left. The landlords were pissed off – they thought I'd been unreasonable. After I left, I heard second-hand, from one of the other performers, that there'd been a fire in the house a hundred years ago or so, and that a little girl had died in the fire.

A few months later, when I was appearing in *Guys and Dolls* at the National Theatre, a friend of mine came to stay in my house in London. Now this friend is a doctor, and I'd say he was quite 'sensitive', in the sense of having psychic abilities. He wasn't a boyfriend or anything, just a house guest, and he was sleeping in the spare room. After that night, he said to me over breakfast, 'Lizzie, I can't sleep in your house. I saw a little girl standing on the threshold of your bedroom, and she's like a little Rottweiler – very protective of you, doesn't want anyone else near.' Now the point is that I hadn't told him anything about the episode in Nottinghamshire, and he could have had no knowledge of the little girl from me.'

[We were speaking by phone early in the evening, and at this point Lizzie broke off, saying, 'You know, I'm sweating like a pig telling you this.']

THE FORMATION OF THE ELEMENTS

When somebody tells my friend David a ghost story, he will never raise an eyebrow at the end and say, 'Are you sure?' He is inclined to believe them... Because why would they lie? Perhaps to entertain, in which case the question becomes, 'Did they succeed?', and if they did, then it doesn't matter either way. There is a virtuous circle in that the more entertaining a ghost story is, the truer it sounds, and vice versa. Fictional and 'true' ghost stories have long since been chasing each other around that circle, and this is the last time you will see those arch inverted commas around the word 'true' and I will try also try to avoid words like 'allegedly' and 'purportedly'. Instead, I will take my cue from a line in 'The Captain of the Pole Star' (1890), an atmospheric if not very frightening ghost story by Arthur Conan Doyle: 'Mr Manson, our second mate, saw a ghost last night – or, at least, says that he did, which of course is the same thing.'

This book concerns itself with both fictional and true ghost stories, and the word 'ghostliness' spans the two. Three writers were particularly important in defining the elements of British ghostliness, which will dictate the structure of the rest of the book. It might be as well to look briefly at the particular kinds of ghostliness they popularised.

Charles Dickens (1812-70)

Just as Dickens was energetic enough not only to produce his vast output of novels, but also to enact them before audiences on his speaking tours, so he both wrote about ghostliness and pursued it in his life. He practised mesmerism, forerunner of hypnotism, which posited the existence of an invisible universal fluid, which could be manipulated by the force of animal magnetism. Directing this force by a waving of hands, and use of his 'visual ray' (staring into the subject's eyes), Dickens could put people into trances in order to soothe their anxieties and ailments. Mesmerism was probably, although its practitioners didn't know it, a by-product of Michael Faraday's work connecting electricity and magnetism.

In his magisterial biography, Peter Ackroyd also asserts that Dickens attended séances, and quotes him as saying, of the supernatural, 'I have always had a strong interest in the subject and never knowingly lose an opportunity of pursuing it.' Ackroyd reports that Dickens 'dreamed of a lady in a red shawl who turned to him and said, "I am Miss Napier."'(A very powerful image, both in its speed and its eroticism). 'The next evening,' Ackroyd continues, 'he met the same lady, wearing the same shawl and bearing the same name.'

In the early summer of 1854, just after he'd finished *Hard Times*, Dickens was walking past the Burlington Hotel when 'I suddenly (the temperature being then most violent) found an icy coolness come upon me, accompanied with a general stagnation of the blood, a numbness of the extremities, great bewilderment of mind, and a vague sense of wonder.' He then recollected that he had had exactly the same experience once before on the same spot. What was the Burlington Hotel is now 19 Cork Street, the site of an art gallery called Browse and Darby. One fine, late spring day I stood outside it for a while to see whether anything happened. I did not find that spot on the pavement to be particularly cold, but then a car drove up; some women climbed out of it and carried lilies into the gallery. Aren't lilies the flowers of the dead? Encouraged, I walked into the gallery, where some pretty good, very English-looking figurative oils were on display. I asked the man behind the desk whether he knew that the place had once been a hotel. He did know. I told him that supernatural phenomena had been detected around the building. 'Who by?' he asked. 'Charles Dickens,' I replied, and he didn't flinch, but just said, 'Well, I've never noticed anything... And I've spent many a night here.'

As a young man Dickens read many Gothic novels.

These promoted atmosphere, and from them, and from his own insecure childhood, Dickens developed his interest in terrible weather, and the counteracting comforts of home and hearth. These moods could be juxtaposed in ghost stories, of which there are two within Dickens's first novel, *The Pickwick Papers* (1837). The second of these, 'The Bagman's Tale', is told around a Christmas fireside, and most of those ghost stories that have a cosy frame – with the narrator urging the landlord to charge the glasses and 'Throw another log on the fire' before settling down to his tale – owe a lot to Dickens.

He did more than anyone to make the British Christmas ghostly, and most of his ghost stories appeared in the Christmas numbers of the magazines he edited: first 'Household Words' and then 'All The Year Round'. Other writers contributed, and Dickens established a sort of production line of ghost story writers that included his friend Wilkie Collins and a team of women, Rosa Mulholland, Amelia Edwards, Mary Elizabeth Braddon, and Rhoda Broughton. He was a man for 'a round of ghost stories around the fire' (to quote the title of the Christmas 1852 number of 'Household Words'), as though they were to be produced as readily and with the same certainty of giving satisfaction as glasses of punch. Dickens's best-known Christmas ghost story, *A Christmas Carol* (1843), does most of the things a ghost story is capable of doing. It has the atmosphere, the sceptical interjections ('It's humbug still!' cries Scrooge, having suffered the opening volley of supernatural effects), the steady mounting of tension, and the small possibility of subjective explanation (Did Scrooge dream it all?) that were becoming established as requirements.

Sheridan Le Fanu (1814-73)

Le Fanu, a relation of Sheridan the playwright, was born into the Anglo-Irish aristocracy. His early ghost stories were widely scattered in Dublin journals, and he became successful in his lifetime as a writer of mystery novels, the best-known being *Uncle Silas*, in which the eponymous villain is demonic but not ghostly. Some of Le Fanu's ghost stories were collected in *Madam Crowl's Ghost and Other Tales of Mystery*, edited in 1923 by M.R. James (very close now – see directly below), who, like Dickens, regarded him highly.

Le Fanu was steeped in Gothic literature and Irish folk myths, the latter being reflected in the appearance of some of his ghosts in animal form. In the best known of his ghost stories, 'Green Tea', a bookish, retiring bachelor-cleric called Mr Jennings is haunted by a small, libidinous monkey, which first appears to him on a bus. He pokes at it with his umbrella, which goes right through it. (Le Fanu is a modern ghost story writer in that his ghosts appear in everyday contexts). It might be that the monkey has biological causes lying in Jennings's addiction to green tea. This has caused the opening of his 'inner eye', which allowed him to perceive the monkey. The notion of the inner eye comes from the Swedish mystic, Swedenborg, who fascinated Victorian ghost story writers, including

Dickens, who wrote to Le Fanu, seeking elucidation on certain of Swedenborg's theories, especially those about exactly how mesmerism might trigger an opening of the inner eye. (Anyone seeking relief from the bustle of the West End might bear a little eastwards, towards Bloomsbury Way, just off New Oxford Street, and The Swedenborg Society Bookshop, which usually has a blackboard outside it, announcing that it is dedicated to 'The Most Extraordinary Person in Recorded History.' I often go in and browse through the books by or about the man. His accounts of his meetings with aliens are particularly interesting. For instance, Swedenborg conversed regularly with a man from Venus, who revealed that the inhabitants of that planet are so markedly different from the people of earth that they actually sleep the opposite way in their beds – with their feet at the head.)

Alternatively, the monkey in Green Tea might be psychological, an emanation of Jennings's id or subconscious. The story is narrated by a Dr Hesselius, a 'medical philosopher' – a psychiatrist, in other words. Great play is made of his scepticism, his intelligence and his learning, and he is much given to saying things like, 'I reserve all that borders on the technical for a scientific paper.'

In having connections with folk myths, and in anticipating the subjective and psychological explanations of later ghost stories, Le Fanu straddles the entire genre. But this would count for nothing if he couldn't frighten, and his 'An Account of Some Strange Disturbances in Aungier Street', published in 1853, is the haunted house that anyone hoping to contribute to the genre has to reckon with.

In that story, two students rent a house in Dublin formerly occupied by a 'hanging judge'. One of the two, lying in bed at night, sees the furniture in his room with a particular intensity. He feels the 'tableau of horror' being mustered. Presently, he finds his attention fixed upon the window opposite the foot of his bed: 'I became somehow conscious of a sort of horrid but undefined preparation going forward in some unknown quarter and by some unknown agency...' After this 'lighting up of the theatre', the first of the 'infernal manifestations' appears: '...a picture suddenly flew up to the window, where it remained fixed, as if by an electrical attraction... The picture thus mysteriously glued to the window-panes was the portrait of an old man, in a crimson flowered silk dressing-gown, the folds of which I could even now describe, with a countenance embodying a strange mixture of intellect, sensuality and power, but withal sinister and full of malignant omen.'

(What clinches this for me is the word 'preparation', the malice aforethought).

Le Fanu himself would sit up in bed anticipating, or trying to conjure, nightmare visions for use in his fiction, and the vision he all too successfully called up involved a large Victorian house collapsing on him as he slept. When he died in bed – of a heart attack and with a shocked expression on his face – his doctor observed, 'That house fell at last'.

At one of our ghost sessions in Vat's Wine Bar, I discussed this aspect of ghostliness with my friend David. I told him that when I go to Scarborough, I can hardly bear to look at the north wall of the vast Grand Hotel, which is totally blank, without the relief of a window – so many bricks (most turned slimy and green by sea spray) that I can't help but imagine what would happen if they came unstuck and fell down. But then The Grand, built in 1863 as one of the world's first purpose-built hotels, is a true haunted house: a monumental anachronism, too large for the modern world, or at least for modern Scarborough. I stayed there once in October, in a room overlooking the dark thrashings of the North Sea (I had paid a five pound supplement for the view), and on neither occasion did I see anyone else on the same corridor, or even the same floor.

That evening, I saw some of the other guests huddled in a corner of the great lobby, near the lights of a little stage located in an alcove, from where bingo numbers were being called by a desperate-sounding voice.

I had a similar sense of being bullied by brickwork in Le Fanu's home city of Dublin, where there are streets of frighteningly big red-brick terraced houses. A haunted terraced house would be inconceivable in an English city but not in Dublin. David heard me out and then, in his pithy way, quoted a line from Alan Bennett's television play about Franz Kafka, *The Insurance Man*, in which Kafka mentions, apropos an accident claim, that bricks don't fall on people in Japan because they have paper houses. He reflects, by contrast, on 'the sheer weight of Prague.'

M.R. James (1862-1936)

Those are his dates, but the more I think of M.R. James the further back in time he seems to recede. Here was a reticent Cambridge don, a biblical scholar, the foremost expert on medieval manuscripts of his time and Provost of both King's College, Cambridge and Eton, where he himself had been a precocious schoolboy, reading for pleasure 'works of the greatest knottiness' ('I am reading Ethiopic,' he wrote home at one point). Here was a godly man, a bespectacled and owlish self-declared 'confirmed bachelor'; a tricyclist and smoker of briar pipes. The biography of him by Richard Pfaff devotes about five pages to James's ghost stories, and the rest to his academic work. It's likely that any future full length biography will be the other way around.

James's *Collected Ghost Stories* has been in print since 1931, and it sets the benchmark for the genre. The stories are economical, dry, droll. His protagonists are upper-middle-class men of sceptical and academic inclinations. Aiming to do some light historical research as a relief from the rigours of term time, they travel to the countryside, usually by implication East Anglia, alighting from an empty train at a deserted station with a bundle of books under their arms, and a faint suspicion of being watched, which of course they immediately dismiss.

While tramping across the countryside, or poking about in a church, they stumble upon medieval artefacts, and are too dismissive of their magic and mystery, instead taking a narrowly rationalist approach to them. They are the kind of men who will walk under ladders, just to see what will happen. They trust too much to their intellects or, like Bluebeard's wife, they are impertinently curious. In 'Count Magus' (1904), Dr Anderson's 'curiosity exceeded his wisdom'. In 'Rats' (1919), Mr Thompson books himself into an inn near the Suffolk coast. A locked room in his corridor, noticed during a break from reading, puts him 'in a mood of indefensible curiosity'. Thompson is 'reduced to inarticulacy' by what he discovers.

James's men are usually not killed by the spirit or demon they unearth, but they are chastened. They will know to leave well alone next time. His protagonists are so like himself, at least by class and profession, that a degree of self-chastisement might be seen in the stories.

M.R. James read his ghost stories to the Eton College scout troupe, or to the choir boys at King's before Midnight Mass on Christmas Eve – for both of which you'd certainly need CRB clearance today – and he spoke of them as mere entertainments. He was often asked whether he believed in ghosts, to which he replied: 'I am prepared to consider evidence and accept it if it satisfies me.' But the sheer, horripilating creepiness of his tales suggests that they came from deep within him. In 'Casting the Runes' (the story on which the film *Night of the Demon* is based), the hero, Dunning, has tangled with Karswell, a sinister expert on diabolic literature. Dunning hears a sound from his study during the night. Getting up to investigate, he encounters nothing but a sudden gust of warm air. He goes back to bed, and reaches for a book kept under his pillow. His hand '...did not get so far. What he touched was, according to his account, a mouth with teeth, and with hair about it, and, he declares, not the mouth of a human being.'

In 1927, in the introduction to a collection called *Ghosts and Marvels*, James deigned to set out 'the qualities which have been observed to accompany success' in ghost stories. The two most valuable elements were 'atmosphere' and a 'nicely managed crescendo'. He wanted to see the characters going about their ordinary business, 'undisturbed by forebodings... and into this calm environment let the ominous thing put out its head, unobtrusively at first, and then more insistently, until it holds the stage.' He also suggested leaving 'a loophole for a natural explanation; but, I would say, let the loophole be so narrow as not to be quite practicable.'

Dickens excelled at atmosphere, Le Fanu at anticipation. James could do both. But they all played by the same rules, and from their writings, and others besides, I have distilled what I consider to be the elements of ghostliness. Buttressed by quotations from my Big Three, these give me the headings for the next three parts of this book, which are:

– 'It's humbug still!' or The Sceptical Point of View

– 'It had not been light all day': Atmosphere.

– 'The lighting up of the theatre' and 'the infernal illusion', or The Crescendo and the Manifestation.

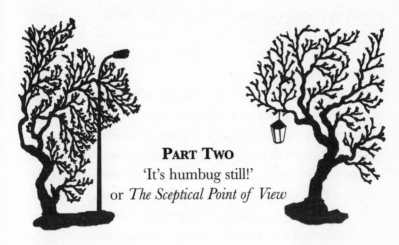

PART TWO
'It's humbug still!'
or *The Sceptical Point of View*

Ghost stories in the modern sense – a description of some anomalous event designed to create a pleasurable shiver – did not exist in medieval times because, to the medieval mind, the whole of life was a ghost story. Except theirs weren't ghosts as we would understand them.

Karen Maitland is the author of two recent, bestselling medieval thrillers: 'The Company of Liars' and 'The Owl Killers' (and if she were about to relate a ghost sighting, I'd also mention that she is in fact Dr Karen Maitland, since she has a Ph.D in psycholinguistics).

At a literary event, where we ought to have been discussing other things, she told me that 'the medieval belief system didn't include disembodied ghosts. Instead a body, or any part of it, could be animated, and it would speak or sing, usually in riddles. It would often tell who its murderer had been. In order to find out information, priests would raise the dead. Necromancy was part of the

Christian religion, but if it was carried out by a lay person then it was witchcraft.'

An account of one such feat of licensed communication with the dead appears in 'The Prioress's Tale' from *The Cantebury Tales*. It is carried out by an Abbott on the body of a young boy murdered by the Jews in the ghetto of 'a Christian town' in Asia. The boy draws attention to his killing by singing praises to God after his death. This is a re-telling of the English legend of Little Sir Hugh of Lincoln, which arose from the disappearance of a boy in that town. The local Jews were blamed for his murder, and nineteen of them were executed over it. In Neville Coghill's translation of The Prioress's Tale, the Abbot proclaims:

'Dear child, I conjure thee
By virtue of the Holy Trinity
To say how singing is permitted thee
Although they throat is cut, or seems to be.'

(The child discloses to the Abbot that he can speak after death by virtue of a grain placed on his tongue by the Virgin Mary).

'The Prioress's Tale' reads as pure anti-Semitism today, but according to Karen Maitland, Chaucer's intention may have been to satirise the Abbot for his necromancy, a practice not to the taste of all Christians of the time.

The other 'ghost story' from *The Canterbury Tales* is 'The Nun Priest's Tale' from which concerns a series of prophetic dreams. One might call that a story of the supernatural, but no such concept existed in Chaucer's time.

The term is a product of the Age of Reason. It signifies some special, unaccountable force operating outside the laws of nature, and this is what ghosts had become by the eighteenth century. They were by now mysterious anomalies perceived at the margins of experience. Accordingly, they assumed a less definite form. They became disembodied, transparent, ethereal.

Given the imponderable, wispy nature of the modern ghost, the narrator of the modern ghost story generally presents himself as sceptical, not prone to fantastical imaginings. If he saw the ghost, the listener is meant to think, then it really must have appeared. So the narrator presents his bona fides: if he does happen to hold a Cycling Proficiency Certificate, or if he got an A-Star in GCSE maths, he will say so.

THE PRESENTING OF CREDENTIALS: FIVE EXAMPLES

1. 'This thing is so rare in all its circumstances, and on so good authority, that my reading and conversation has not given me anything like it. It is fit to gratify the most ingenious and serious inquirer. Mrs Bargrave is the person to whom Mrs Veal appeared after her death; she is my intimate friend, and I can avouch for her reputation for these last fifteen or sixteen years...' So begins what has been called, by virtue of its cool and sceptical tone, the first modern ghost story (and yes, its title is meant to be written in lower case): 'A true relation of the apparition of one Mrs Veal the next day after her death to one Mrs Bargrave at Canterbury the 8th of September, 1705', by Daniel Defoe.

2. 'Thirty years ago, an elderly man to whom I paid quarterly a small annuity charged on some property of mine, came on the quarter-day to receive it. He was a dry, sad, quiet man, who had known better days, and had always maintained an unexceptionable character. No better character could be imagined for a ghost story.' From 'Mr Justice Harbottle' (1872) by Sheridan Le Fanu. (Or see, from the beginning of 'The Authentic Narrative of a Ghost of a Hand', by the same author: 'I'm sure she believed every word she related, for old Sally was veracious.')

3. 'My reader is to make the most that can reasonably be made of my feeling jaded, having a depressing sense upon me of a monotonous life, and being "slightly dyspeptic". I am assured by my renowned doctor that my real state of health at that time justifies no stronger description, and I quote his own from his written answer to my request for it.' From 'To Be Taken with a Grain of Salt' (also known as 'The Trial for Murder'), by Charles Dickens, published in 1865. Dickens practically gives his narrator a signed certificate of sanity. This is almost bullying the reader; tantamount to saying: 'If you don't believe the following, *you* must be mad.'

4. '...and I feel bound to tell you, Mr Otis, that the ghost has been seen by several living members of my family, as well as by the rector of the parish, the Revd August Dampier, who is a Fellow of King's College, Cambridge.' Lord Canterville, speaking in 'The Canterville Ghost' by Oscar Wilde (1887). This is a joke ghost story, admittedly.

5. 'I am not mad.' The start of 'Sealskin Trousers' by Eric Linklater, published in 1947.

When our friends tell us their true stories, they use similar devices: 'I've no time for ghosts normally, but there was this one occasion...' It's more fun like that. Nobody wants to listen someone who begins, 'And the sixteenth time I saw a ghost...' or to read a ghost story narrated by a character who, like the Satanist in 'My Black Mirror' by Wilkie Collins (1856), gleefully declares: 'I have not one morsel of rationality about me.' (While that story is an effective mood piece it goes nowhere and lacks tension).

It should be mentioned that the writer, in making his main character sceptical, is having his cake and eating it. On the one hand, the character's scepticism makes the story more credible; but at the same time, the writer usually disapproves of this scepticism, and will make the character pay for it. As Le Fanu writes in 'An Account of Some Strange Disturbances in Aungier Street', 'The sceptic is destined to receive a lesson'. The writer is on the side of the ghosts after all. If he is a ghost story specialist he makes his entire living from them, so why wouldn't he be? Each avowal of scepticism provokes fate and increases tension.

And sometimes the effect is underlined by the protagonist's dismissal of warnings from people who may be unsophisticated but do possess local knowledge.

THREE YOKELS WHO TURNED OUT TO BE RIGHT

1. In the much-anthologised story, 'The Monkey's Paw'
(1902) by W.W. Jacobs, the bluff sergeant major, back from
twenty years in India, visits the slightly more genteel White
family (husband, wife and son) in their cottage one evening.
He produces from his pocket a withered monkey's paw. 'It
had a spell put on it by a fakir,' he announces, 'He wanted
to show that fate ruled people's lives, and that those who
interfered with it did so to their sorrow. He put a spell on
it so that three separate men could each have three wishes
from it.' He then pitches it into the fire, but Mr White
fishes it out, curious about the wishes. 'Better let it burn,'
says the sergeant major. 'If you keep it, don't blame me for
what happens.' 'The idea of our listening to such nonsense!' says Mrs White when he's gone. By this time, however, Mr White has made his wishes, only slightly per-
turbed by the way the piano gave a sudden crash, and the
paw seemed to twist in his hand as he did so.

2. In 'Dracula's Guest', by Bram Stoker (1914), the narrator forsakes the comforts of his hotel, the Quatre Saisons
in Munich, in favour of a walk in the countryside, this
even though it is Walpurgis Nacht, when the demons walk.
Presently, he and his German coachman, Johann, come to

a junction where the narrator is minded to walk down a certain lane...

'"Tell me," I said, "about this place where the road leads," and I pointed down.' Johann crosses himself and mutters, "It is unholy."' Pressed further, he jabbers something about a graveyard, from which sounds are heard at night. Finally, in an agony of desperation, he cries "*Walpurgis Nacht!*" and points at the coach urging the narrator to get in.

But all the narrator's English blood rises at this: '"You are afraid, Johann – you are afraid. Go home; I shall return alone; the walk will do me good."'

A little while later, standing in the middle of a thunderstorm which has appeared from nowhere, and looking at a huge marble sepulchre that is marked with the legend 'The Dead Travel Fast', and which has an iron spike driven clean through it, the narrator 'began to wish for the first time that I had listened to Johann's advice.'

3. In 'The Judge's House' (1914), also by Bram Stoker, Malcolm Malcolmson, a mathematics student, decides to rent a 'rambling, heavy-built house in the Jacobean style' in order to prepare for an examination. It is 'unusually small' (and yet still massive), and surrounded by a high brick wall. When the wife of the local inn-keeper hears of this plan, she exclaims, 'Not in the judge's house!' and grows pale. She would not take 'all the money in Drinkwater's Bank' (whatever that is) to stay in the house herself. 'If you were my boy – and you'll excuse me for saying it – you wouldn't sleep there a night, not if I had to go there myself and pull the big alarm bell that's on that roof!'

Malcolmson is amused, but also touched by her concern: 'A man who is reading for the Mathematical Tripos has too much to think of to be disturbed by any of these mysterious "somethings", and his work is of too exact and prosaic a kind to allow of his having any corner of his mind for mysteries of this kind.'

But this is not the last we will hear of that alarm bell on the roof.

ALL OUR YESTERDAYS

It is almost a ghostly thrill in itself to encounter a clever and plausible person willing to give ghosts the benefit of the doubt. I would put my father into that category. (He passed his Eleven Plus, can do mental arithmetic faster than anyone I've known, and rose high in the financial side of British Railways, North Eastern Region). He was – and is – a man with a cynical front, who used to say that those of my friends who appeared over-whimsical or dreamy were 'a bit soft'. And yet he himself was named John after a ghost.

This came about as follows...

As a girl, my father's mother, lying in bed in Newcastle in mid-1916, had been visited by a vision of her brother, John, who had said, 'You won't see me again, so I'm coming to say goodbye.' He was reported killed in action on the Western Front the next week. My father's mother had shared a bed with her sister, and both had seen and heard the spirit, technically known as a 'crisis apparition' or 'death wraith'. My paternal grandmother died more or less at the moment of my birth, so I never met her, but my father says that she was 'nobody's fool', and if *he's* anything to go by then she certainly wasn't.

My father used to point me towards the TV appearances of a man called Brian Inglis, who died in 1993 and was, like my father, interested in the supernatural. When I was a boy Inglis presented a programme with the fascinatingly dreary title, *All Our Yesterdays*. It showed newsreel clips of wars, political crises, and natural disasters from twenty-five years before, and Inglis, a reserved, donnish figure, commented elegantly upon them. He was an author – the profession I aspired to – and had been the editor of *The Spectator*, which I used to read for self-improvement in the reference section of York Library, so his qualifications could hardly have been higher in my eyes. Every time I watched him on tv, I thought, 'This man believes in ghosts', and it was a challenge to my own scepticism.

My father told me that Inglis's interest in the supernatural had begun by his reading of the precognitive dreams of J.W. Dunne. Dunne himself had an impressive CV, having designed the first military aircraft which actually got off the ground....which was just as well, since his claim was that he dreamed things that then happened. In 1902, while serving in South Africa with the 6th Mounted Light Infantry, and sleeping in a small settlement that had just been heavily shelled by the Boers, he dreamed of a volcano erupting on an island, with major loss of life. He then saw himself – in his dream – on a neighbouring island pleading for assistance in French, and addressing 'Monsieur le Maire'. Four weeks later he read in 'The Daily Telegraph': 'Volcano Disaster in Martinique – Town Swept Away – An Avalanche of Flames', and he realised that this event had occurred twenty-four hours after his dream. Moreover the council and mayor of the neigh-bouring island, St Lucia, spoke French patois.

In 1977 and 1984, Inglis published two books, *Natural and Supernatural* and *Science and Parascience*, which told the story of the great battle between the believers and the sceptics that waged between the mid-nineteenth and the mid-twentieth century. They were passed on to me by my father, and I recall that the critics accused Inglis of being too credulous. Certainly, he is generous towards the believ-ers in the books. For instance, he mentions that both mete-orites and lightning were once regarded as supernatural, and that one apparently supernatural phenomenon, mes-merism, gave rise to hypnotism, which has found its way into orthodox medicine.

I mention Inglis because he was a conundrum to me. Given the nature of his beliefs he couldn't be right; but his character so impressed me that he couldn't be wrong either – at least not wholly. And even if he was partly right, then I would have to remake my whole world view. He was a symbol of the imponderability of the questions to do with the supernatural. When I was mulling these over, in the 1980's, not many others were similarly occupied. But these questions had divided British society for the past century and more.

THE SCEPTICS AND THE SPIRITUALISTS

Before Spiritualism there was mesmerism. That was the first dividing line. We have seen that in the theories of the Swedish visionary Emanuel Swedenborg, mesmerism could lead to clairvoyance by the opening of the 'inner eye', and in this way mesmerism became ghostly. A story called 'The Haunters and The Haunted', published in 1859 by Edward Bulwer-Lytton, sometime Conservative cabinet minister, Peer of the Realm, friend of Dickens, and the most successful British writer of the mid-nineteenth century, is an attempt to show mesmerism – sometimes referred to by Bulwer-Lytton simply as 'electricity' – as the cause of ghosts. The visions seen in the haunted house of the story, located somewhere just north of Oxford Street, are projections from the mind of a malevolent mesmeric genius. But when that story was published, the psychological subtleties of mesmerism were being displaced by something more literal: the attempt to contact the dead through Spiritualism

Spiritualism came to Britain from America where, in the early 1850's, a pair of sisters, Margaret and Kate Fox, seemed to be channelling ghosts in a house near Rochester in New York State. The spirit communicated by rapping on a table, or moving objects, including the table itself;

chairs were pulled from under sitters, musical instruments played by invisible means. The channelling of spirits was not in itself new. One of its ancient roots lay in the oracles, those places or people from which prophecies emanate. The oracles of Ancient Greece were frequently seeresses, or Sybils, and they would go into disturbing trances when downloading their spirit messages, just like the Victorian mediums, who were predominantly women.

The ambassadress of Spiritualism to Britain was another American female medium, Mrs W.R. Hayden, wife of a New England newspaper proprietor. Her spirits confined themselves to rapping, and she impressed by her sober demeanour and her intelligence. (She later qualified as a doctor). It was noted with approval that she was always seated at some distance from the tables on which the raps were made. Augustus de Morgan, first holder of the Chair of Mathematics at University College London, tested her when she came to Britain. He brought her into his own home, and the raps spelled out the name of an obscure academic periodical that would have been known only to Mr de Morgan's dead father, and very few others.

And so the battle between the sceptics and Spiritualists was joined. It was provoked by the advancement of science, and the publication in 1859 of 'On the Origin of Species' by Charles Darwin. Where did that leave life after death? In reply the believers tried to give the only irrefutable answer: the production of an actual spirit. For some, the production of a verifiable spirit would mean proof of Christianity, although the Church did not require any such proof, and was embarrassed about the business of seeking it. It had its own licensed angels, thank you very much, and did not want to extend the franchise.

The battleground was the séance room, and 'the media', in the mid-nineteenth century, meant the mediums who could contact 'the other side'. If you live in a large Victorian house, it is likely that a séance was at some point held in one of its rooms. Go into, say, the dining room, and imagine those people who tried so hard to see what lies 'beyond the veil', and who have now gone beyond it themselves, and so presumably know. Picture the ghosts of the ghost-hunters. The circular table is perhaps an antique, dating from those days. Picture, seated around that table, a group of respectable looking people in evening wear. The room is in semi-darkness – illuminated, if at all, by red-shaped lamps. Those assembled – the 'sitters' – are holding hands in a way that seems at odds with the formality of their clothing, and they are focused upon one of their number, a person looking perhaps slightly less respectable than the others. This is the medium or 'sensitive', and he or she – more often a she, since men are generally *not* very sensitive – is in a trance state while attempting to channel messages to the sitter from the other side.

Quite often no messages came through, which was like going to a football match and seeing a nil-nil draw. When the messages did come, they might be 'written' out by a planchette – a pen on wheels lightly held by all the sitters, and supposedly capable of writing without conscious direction. They might be encoded in tappings on the table, or they might come directly from the mouth of the medium, in a voice evidently not his or her own, which made people wonder whether mediums were really ventriloquists...

...And were they highly skilled magicians as well? Because at a really successful demonstration of what was called 'physical mediumship' the séance was less a muted chamber piece and more a full-blown symphony. There might be ectoplasm: a luminous white stuff oozing from the medium and resembling in texture old toothpaste. Sitters were warned not to touch any that might appear, for fear of causing some psychic or physical crisis for the medium. Ectoplasm was either the very essence of ghostliness, a sort of umbilical cord connecting life and death, or it was...well, twisted linen covered in phosphorous.

Everyday objects might appear in the room from nowhere – these were called apports. Things – trumpets, flowers – levitated or flew about the room, including sometimes the very substantial table, or even the medium him or herself; and sometimes – the ultimate coup de théâtre – another person entirely appeared, which is to say: a ghost.

To prove that they were dead, the spirits had to prove that they had been alive. They might do this by revealing themselves to be phantoms of the eminent; or dead friends or relatives of the deceased. Everyone at the sitting would have known something of the eminent figures, while a few – perhaps just one sitter – would know a great deal about the purported friend or relative. So either strategy had its risks for the fraudulent medium.

'By the spring of 1853,' writes Brian Inglis in *Natural and Supernatural*, 'table-tilting had become the fashionable social pastime, even in the Royal residence at Osborne, where the table moved for Victoria and Albert. Under Lady Ely's hands it fairly rushed about, convincing Victoria that it was no trick, or illusion: magnetism, she thought, or electricity must be responsible.' Inglis reports a séance attended by the historian Thomas Macaulay. He had started as a sceptic, but was forced to admit that there was 'rotary motion' of the table. He could not see how this might be happening, unless the man opposite him, the Bishop of Oxford, Samuel Wilberforce, had done the pushing.

Take down from the shelf the biography of your favourite nineteenth-century luminary and look in the index under 'Spiritualism' or 'Supernatural' or 'occult'. There will almost certainly be an entry.

FOUR EMINENT SÉANCE-GOERS.

1. Anthony Trollope

In *Anthony Trollope: A Victorian in his World*, Richard Mullen records that, in 1840, when he was twenty-five, Trollope was struck down by a mysterious and protracted illness. His mother, Fanny, called in her own doctor, John Elliotson, who had been doctor to both Dickens and Thackeray, and who had taught Dickens mesmerism. (But he was also –

mockers take note – the first doctor to use a stethoscope). He gave public demonstrations, in which he practised mesmerism on two particularly receptive subjects, or 'somnambules': the Okey sisters. As part of their psychic repertoire, the sisters could predict the chances of a patient recovering according to whether or not they saw a figure called Jack standing by his side. Fanny Trollope, who was interested in the supernatural, asked Elliotson to bring them to Anthony's bedside to find out whether they could see Jack.

They could, but only up to the top of his boots, which meant that Anthony would recover.

Anthony Trollope inherited his mother's interest in the supernatural, but with a stronger dose of scepticism. He attended at least one séance given by the golden boy of British mediumship, Daniel Dunglas Home (see below). It was in Ealing. Trollope later wrote: 'Men who cannot believe in the mystery of our Saviour's redemption can believe that spirits from the dead have visited them in a stranger's parlour, because they see a table shake and do not know how it is shaken; because they hear a rapping on a board, and cannot see the instrument that raps it...' He found these manifestations 'unworthy of the previous grand ceremony of death. Your visitor from above or below should be majestical, should stalk in all panoplied from head to foot – at least in a white sheet, and should not condescend to catechetical and alphabetical puzzles.'

In *The Claverings* (1867), the two upper-class twits, Archie and Doodles, speculate while playing billiards about a medium called Madame Gardeloup: 'If I were a spirit I wouldn't go to a woman with such dirty stockings as she had on.'

2. Charles Dickens

At the start of Dickens's story, *The Haunted House* (1862), the protagonist boards a London-bound train in the north at midnight. He sits opposite a goggle-eyed man who is perpetually staring at the back of the compartment 'as though it were a hundred miles off' while taking notes. After some tentative enquiries, the narrator works out that his fellow passenger 'might be what is popularly called a Rapper: one of a sect for (some of) whom I have the highest respect, but whom I don't believe in.' The man explains that he has 'passed the whole night – as indeed I pass the whole of my time now – in spiritual intercourse...'

'The conferences of the night began,' continued the gentleman, turning several leaves of his note-book, 'with this message: 'Evil communications corrupt good manners.'

'Sound,' said I; 'but absolutely new?'

'New from spirits,' returned the gentleman.

I could only repeat my rather snappish, 'Oh!' and ask if I might be favoured with the last communication.

'A bird in the hand,' said the gentleman, reading his last entry with great solemnity, 'is worth two in the Bosh.'

'Truly I am of the same opinion," said I; "but

shouldn't it be "Bush"'?'

'It came to me "Bosh,"' returned the gentleman.'

According to the stranger, there are seventeen thousand four hundred and seventy-nine spirits in the railway carriage, 'but you cannot see them'. They included Pythagoras, and John Milton who had repudiated the authorship of *Paradise Lost* and 'had introduced, as joint authors of that poem, two unknown gentlemen, respectively named Grungers and Scadingtone.'

3. Arthur Conan Doyle

Speaking as a writer of crime fiction, I would find Doyle insufferable if he'd just gone about basking in the glory of his unbeatable Sherlock Holmes stories. Instead, he proved his imaginative genius by creating that ruthlessly sceptical 'desiccated calculating machine' Holmes, while he himself was able to believe in almost anything. As Michael Coren writes in his biography of the man, 'For the last ten years of his life Conan Doyle effectively became the missionary-in-chief of world Spiritualism' – which he regarded as 'the basis for all religious improvement' of 'a thoroughly material generation'.

Doyle had been converted in the mid-1880's by Alfred Drayson, a distinguished solider, mathematician and astronomer. (In tribute to Drayson, the master-criminal Moriarty – Sherlock Holmes's intellectual rival and nemesis – is both a mathematician and astronomer).

Doyle became a regular séance-goer. In 1918 he

attended, in France, a séance given by Eva C, who was the most famous medium in the world at the time, and vouched for by Professor Charles Richet, winner of the Nobel Prize for medicine in 1913. Eva C's trademark was the production of ectoplasm, and by special dispensation, Doyle was allowed to touch the stuff: 'The ectoplasm I saw upon Eva, the much-abused medium, took the form of a six-inch gelatinous material across the lower portion of the front of her dress. Speaking as a medical man, I should say that it was more like a section of umbilical cord, but it was wider and softer. I was permitted to touch it, and I felt it thrill and contract between my fingers.'

Doyle's son, Innes, had died of pneumonia contracted at the battle of the Somme. Doyle felt that he had re-encountered the boy at séances, and so he became the figurehead of the Spiritualistic wave that followed the war. His book of 1918, *The New Revelation* revealed, according to 'The Times', an 'incredible naiveté', and Doyle did seem infinitely credulous. For instance, he believed it might be possible for him to collaborate on literary works with the spirits of Charles Dickens, Oscar Wilde and Joseph Conrad. (How could that have worked contractually, I wonder?)

He also endorsed the Cottingley Fairies.

In 1920, fifteen-year old Elsie Wright, and her cousin, ten-year old Frances Griffiths, claimed to have seen fairies dancing at the edge of a beck at Cottingley near Bradford, and produced photographs taken by Elsie to prove it. The fairies in the picture looked suspiciously fairy-like, but

Doyle believed the girls. (Some sixty years later, Frances said, 'From where I was I could see the hatpins holding up the figures. I've always marvelled that anybody ever took it seriously.')

Nothing takes away from Conan Doyle's moral integrity, but his gullibility undermines the sceptical assertions of the characters in the handful of ghost stories that he wrote. The narrator in 'The Captain of the Pole-Star' condemns the 'absurd outbreak of superstition' among a ship's crew given to 'spectral alarms'. This is hard to take from a man who believed that the Wright-Griffiths fairies merited an immediate public enquiry.

4. Arthur Balfour

Balfour was the languid, aesthetic and cynical Conservative Prime Minister of 1902-1905. My father used to quote with approval Balfour's characteristic utterance: 'Nothing matters very much, and most things don't matter at all.' Yet he was curious about the supernatural. At times of political crisis, he could generally be found either stretched on a sofa reading a novel, playing golf, or dabbling in trying to contact the dead. From 1875, he arranged séances with a variety of mediums at his home at 4 Carlton Gardens SW1. In 1896, he became the President of the Society for Psychical Research (see below), a move that would be inadvisable in any rising politician of today. In *Arthur James Balfour*, Kenneth Young quotes Balfour's as writing: 'On July 30th 1911 Mrs B came to dinner at Carlton Gardens to talk occult with Gerald and me.'

Young observes: 'This was at the height of the constitutional crisis.'

THE HIGH POINT OF BRITISH SPIRITUALISM

Daniel Dunglas Home was the most convincing medium or Victorian times and possibly any other. He was fabled for his ability to levitate while in touch with the spirits.

His portrait hangs above the fireplace in the lecture hall of the College of Psychic Studies in Kensington, which was established at the height of Spiritualism, and of which more later, but for now I will mention that I was given a tour of the College by its administrator a few years ago, and when we were on the third floor she pointed at one tall window and said, 'That's the window that Daniel Dunglas Home flew out of during a séance...' We then walked up to the fifth floor, where she pointed to another window: 'And that,' she said, 'is the one he came back in by.' There are several other buildings in London where the same stories are told.

D.D. Home was born in Scotland in 1833, the illegitimate product of the family that would give us the Conservative Prime Minister, Alec Douglas Home. Like the Prime Minister, Home pronounced his name 'Hume' but he was above such worldly concerns, or did a good job of appearing to be so. He was raised by an aunt in Connecticut, America, where he predicted the death of his closest friend, and his own mother. Unexplained rapping noises began to occur in his presence, and at nineteen he levitated for the first time. His aunt kicked him out of the house, and he stayed for a while with a Swedenborgian minister called George Bush. He began to give séances in America, and his trademark was the appearance of floating disembodied hands.

In 1855 he sailed to England – for his heath, oddly enough. (He was tubercular). He lived in Cox's Hotel in Jermyn Street, whose proprietor was sympathetic to spiritualism. The above-mentioned Edward Bulwer-Lytton was at one of Home's early London séances: the table levitated, one of the hands appeared, and an accordion was played in mid-air. What Bulwer-Lytton saw influenced the ghost stories he would write. The poet Robert Browning and his poetess wife Elizabeth attended another of Home's séances, and also left highly impressed. But soon afterwards, Robert Browning decided he did not believe what he had seen; that trickery must have been involved. For example, the apparent sounds of table rapping could have been caused Home's dislocation and relocation of his toe joints. In 1864, Browning published his famous anti-Spiritualist poem, 'Mr Sludge the Medium':

As for religion – why, I served it, sir!
I'll stick to that! With my phenomena
I laid the atheist sprawling on his back,
Propped up St Paul, or, at least Swedenborg!
In fact, it's just the proper way to baulk
These troublesome fellows – liars, one and all,
Are not these sceptics? Well, to baffle them,

No use in being squeamish: lie yourself!

...which Home could afford to shrug off, since he was by now the golden boy of British Spiritualism: an intelligent, good-looking, thoroughly presentable young man who gave his demonstrations free (although this is not to say that he did not receive payment in kind), and was willing to do so in a good light (although he did prefer darkness).

He seems to have had a sort of willowy, fey charm. Conan Doyle, a fan – and, of course, a medical man – described him as 'blue-eyed and auburn haired, of a type which is peculiarly liable to the attack of tubercule, and the extreme emaciation of his face showed how little power remained within him by which he might resist it.' He was a frock-coated David Bowie, in short.

Home moved for a while to Florence, where he levitated a table for Napoleon III. On returning to England in 1859, he gave a series of weekly high society séances at the behest of Mrs Milner Gibson, wife of the President of the Board of Trade. And in the mid-1860's, he embarked on a run of well-lit, closely documented and monitored séances for Lord Adare, an army officer and journalist, and his father Lord Dunraven, astrologer and archaeologis. Phenomena continued to occur. Home levitated, disembodied voices muttered while he talked (so it couldn't have been ventriloquism), and Lord Adare reported that, while lying down, Home 'elongated' by eight to ten inches, and then 'sank to some eight or ten inches below his normal stature'. (The Sybils of Ancient Egypt had been said to elongate while entranced).

In a lecture of 1866, Home gave what might be regarded as a politically correct defence of his work. 'I believe in my heart that this power is being spread more and more every day to bring us nearer to God. You ask if it makes us purer? My only answer is that we are but mortals, and as such liable to err; but it does teach that the pure in heart shall see God. It teaches that He is love, and that there is no death.'

Home now attracted the attention of the distinguished scientist Sir William Crookes, who, as we shall see, was also involved in the Low Point of British Spiritualism. In 1861 Crookes had discovered the chemical element thallium; he was a fellow of the Royal Society, and editor of the Quarterly Journal of Science, and he looked like a distinguished scientist to the point of parody: lean face, abundant white hair, high forehead, small round glasses. He subjected Home to a 'scientific appraisal' and in 1871 published in his journal reports of tests upon Home that he had conducted along with a Dr William Huggins, another fellow of the Royal Society, and with Serjeant Cox, a barrister sitting in to observe. An accordion enclosed in a cage was observed to play. Home made a pointer turn without touching it.

In the late 1870's, Home retired from mediumship. He was never caught out in any trickery, and a sceptic might say that this was his main achievement. Two magicians of the time – Canti and Bosco – who attended his séances could not say how the phenomena were produced. More than a hundred people attested in writing to having seen him levitate.

THE LOW POINT OF BRITISH SPIRITUALISM

If Daniel Dunglas Home was the golden boy, his female counterpart, for a while, was Florence Cook. She was born, in the East End of London, in 1856, and first 'turned' a table at a tea party when she was aged fifteen. She went on to a career in mediumship. Like D.D. Home, she was good-looking, nicely spoken, willing, in certain circumstances, to perform in good light. She also would not take money for her séances, in which the masochistic element of female mediumship was strongly present. The spirits would pull at her dress, or remove it entirely. In order to prove that her effects were achieved by purely spiritual means she would ask to be tied up inside a cabinet, and I'm sure there was no shortage of Victorian gentlemen willing to go about the task.

Imagine the cabinet as a sort of Punch and Judy booth, with a small 'stage' at the top. Here palely glowing, ghostly faces would manifest themselves between gauze curtains – in particular the face of a spirit identified as Katie King. As a spirit, Katie King had 'form'. She had manifested in American séances in the 1850's, identifying herself as the daughter of a pirate called Henry Morgan, who died in Jamaica in 1688, and who himself had manifested at séances – first in Ohio in 1852.

By 1873, Florence Cook's bravado and/or her psychic powers had increased to the point at which she was capable of producing full figure manifestations of Katie King. While Florence was still, as far as the sitters could tell, tied up inside the cabinet, Katie King would walk the séance room in white robes. On December 9th 1873, Cook was giving a séance hosted by the Earl and Countess of Caithness, and Katie King duly appeared. Now it was considered a breach of etiquette for any sitter to attempt to touch any manifestation. But on this occasion a young man called William Volckman was crass enough to grab hold of Katie King's wrist, which turned out to be very palpable, and attempt to drag her towards a source of light. There was a struggle. Some of the other sitters came to Katie King's aid, and Volckman got a bloodied nose. A man called Henry Dumphy, one of those omnipresent monitoring barristers, asserted that Katie King escaped from Volckman with an uncanny leaping motion reminiscent of a seal, but Volckman argued that there was nothing incorporeal or even seal-like about her.

Since it would have been difficult for Florence Cook to smuggle an accomplice into the séance room, the suspicion among the sceptics had always been that Katie King was in fact Florence Cook, and the two did look similar. But when the cabinet was checked after Volckman's lunge, Florence Cook was found to be still there, still tied in ropes, and with the signet ring of the Earl of Caithness, which had been used as a seal on one of the knots, still in place. Her clothes were apparently in slight disarray, but it was the reputation of Volckman that really suffered. His action was ungallant to begin with, and his account of it was made questionable by the discovery that he was engaged to be married to medium who was a rival of Cook.

At this point, the above-mentioned William Crookes, his interest piqued by his experiments on D.D. Home, turned his scientific beam on Florence Cook. He arranged a séance at his own home, at which Katie appeared, graciously taking Crookes's arm, and showing him the medium, lying in a trance behind the curtain that had, in this case, taken the place of the cabinet. Crookes, a married man, then created a society scandal by moving Florence into his house.

She and he and the ghost formed a strange ménage. It was rumoured that Katie King would walk about the house for hours, quite outside séance conditions. Crookes was given to holding her hand and embracing her when she did appear. He noted that while she was similar in appearance to Cook, there were significant differences. For example, Cook's ears were pierced, whereas Katy's were not. He took fifty-five photographs of Katie King in his house. The originals were destroyed by his heirs, but one famous surviving copy shows Crookes arm in arm with Katie King, and Cook standing to one side with her face wrapped in a shroud considered by Crookes to be ecto-plasmic.

Oddly enough, Katie King's palpability made it more rather than less likely that she was a genuine spirit as far as

Crookes was concerned. But it has been suggested that being in close company with Florence and Katie, who were both attractive young women, even if one of them was theoretically dead, put him in a sort of erotic daze.

Florence Cook's reputation, and that of mediumship in general, was further undermined in 1880 when, after a period of retirement, she began channelling a new young female ghost: Marie. It was as if the assault of Volckman seven years before had set a precedent, and Florence Cook's spirits had become fair game, because another bounder, by the name of Sir George Sitwell, grabbed Marie at a séance held on January 9th 1880. She was discovered to be Florence Cook, wearing her underwear and a flannel petticoat. After this, Cook was damaged goods, even though she would occasionally still produce Marie for séance goers, and it was reported that she could do this while not only tied up in the cabinet or behind a curtain but with a gentleman-observer tied to her.

SPIRITUALISM AND RADIO

William Crookes wrote to Florence Cook's family in 1904 expressing his sincerest sympathy at the news of her death. As far as I know she has not been heard of, or from, since, but Katie King is reported to have manifested at a séance held in Rome in 1974.

Crookes himself teamed up with another medium, Rosina Showers, whose mediumship was as implausible as her name – in fact a genuine one – somehow suggests.

Even though she failed the scientific tests that Crookes subjected her to, he found that 'the evidence in her favour is very strong.'

She then admitted that she'd been faking. Crookes offered a deal: he would not expose her if she gave up the cheating, and this was misinterpreted by Rosina Showers' mother as an attempt at blackmail with a sexual motive. Mrs Showers began circulating scandalous stories about Crookes, in response to which he started a legal action, which he withdrew on receipt of a written retraction from Mrs Showers.

And then Crookes finally gave up on Spiritualism. He wrote to the irreproachable D.D. Home, who was now cutting a very lonely figure as the last untainted medium, that 'were it not for the regard we bear you, I would cut the whole Spiritual connection, and never read, speak, or think of the subject again.' He went back to science, and notwithstanding his embarrassments at the hands of the spiritualists, he was knighted in 1897, and awarded the Order of Merit in 1910. He died in 1919.

William Crookes's work with vacuum tubes would prove important in the development of electronics and radio systems, the scientific writers inform me. In his book on the development of radio, *Signor Marconi's Magic Box*, Gavin Weightman observes that 'Crookes had predicted with remarkable foresight the development of wireless telegraphy up to the point Marconi had taken it by 1901': 'Rays of light will not pierce through a wall, nor, as we know only too well, through a London fog; but electrical vibrations of a yard or more in wave-length will easily pierce such media, which to them will be transparent. Here is revealed the bewildering possibility of telegraphy without wires, posts, cables or any of our present day appliances...'

Another brilliantly imaginative scientist and over-credulous psychic researcher of the time was Oliver Joseph Lodge, who had been educated in spiritualism by his aunt, who he believed returned to speak to him in a séance after her death from cancer. In 1881, he became the first Professor of Physics at Liverpool University. He was a pioneer of X-rays, and the inventor of an electro-magnetic means of collecting dust in factories. The parallels between psychic research and the development of wireless telegraphy – the fascination with invisible means of communication – are even more evident in Lodge's case, since he and Marconi were once neck and neck in the race to be recognised as the begetter of radio. But Lodge's mind was on higher, or still higher, things. Gavin Weightman writes: 'The distinguished former rival of Marconi, Sir Oliver Lodge, had continued his pursuit of the spirits while Marconi was discovering the power of short waves, which cracked the problem of daytime transmission at a distance.'

The problem referred to here was that long radio waves had been found to travel further in the night time. Weightman dryly observes that Marconi's breakthrough 'finally put paid to the theory of the writer Sir Arthur Conan Doyle... that the greater distances achieved by

Marconi at night were proof of the mysterious "powers of darkness" which spiritualist mediums exploited.' (But I have no right to laugh at Doyle, not having the remotest idea how radio waves work. For all I know, a text message might be sent by supernatural means, and when I look along a railway carriage, at all the passengers staring in awe at their mobile phone handsets, I can't believe I'm alone.)

SCEPTICISM TRIUMPHS: SPIRITUALISM IN THE TWENTIETH CENTURY

As already stated, the First World War brought a commercial boom for the spiritualists. When Rudyard Kipling's son, John (or Jack, as he was known), was killed at the Battle of Loos in September 1915, Kipling was bombarded with the calling cards of mediums. Spiritualism was becoming an industry, and increasingly viewed with distaste.

The above-mentioned Oliver Lodge did nothing for the cause with the publication of his book, *Raymond: Or Life and Death*, an account of his re-connection, via Spiritualism, with the eldest of his six sons (he also had six daughters). One medium reported, on behalf of Raymond, 'He lives in a house – a house built of bricks – and there are trees and flowers and the ground is solid. And if you kneel down in the mud, apparently you get your clothes soiled...' and so ploddingly on.

While it might be at the peak of its popularity as a form

of therapy, Spiritualism had lost its intellectual credibility by the 1920s, and the psychical researchers were more concerned with thought transference or telepathy, as we shall see. There had been too many scandals, and the standard response of the believers – that any genuine medium might be driven to fakery once in a while by the pressure to produce results – had been heard too often. As Dickens and Trollope had pointed out, the spirits, when contacted, seldom said or did anything original, or even vaguely interesting. The shades of dead First World War soldiers would send their best wishes to friends and family, signing off with a wish for world peace. Could it be that banality was the defining characteristic of the dead? The defence was not attempted.

Spiritualism declined gently throughout the century, and sank from being a pursuit of society drawing rooms to a much humbler, more suburban business. The last time it was newsworthy was in 1944, when an overweight, not-at-all-ethereal-looking Scottish medium called Helen Duncan was prosecuted under the Witchcraft Act of 1735.

At a séance given in Portsmouth in 1941, Duncan had channelled a young sailor who said that his ship, HMS Barham, had been sunk. Or at least, he might have said that, because accounts of the séance were blurred. HMS Barham *had* been sunk, but the government had not yet released the information. Her Spiritualist defenders argued that Duncan was prosecuted for being right, but the Home Office considered her profession bad for morale, and she was given ten months in Holloway. By now spiritualism was a music hall joke, or would have been if the music halls hadn't also been dying. Whereas the sceptics once challenged the spiritualists, often in the hope of ceasing to be sceptical, they now mocked them.

THREE SATIRES ON SPIRITUALISM

1. In the film *London Belongs to Me*, directed by Sidney Gilliat in 1938 but not released until ten years later, Alistair Sim plays a seedy medium called Mr Squales. He is a sepulchral figure, with a single dyed-black lock of hair. He affects an other-worldy manner. He says that he has 'no thoughts for food' but when offered a plate of bacon and eggs gets through it at lightning speed while cackling delightedly. He lives on commissions to 'give the voice' at seances in south London, where lobster paste sandwiches are served – or at least what purport to be lobster paste sandwiches. But he has to supplement his income by hocking his belongings. Given notice by his landlady, he leaves the rent on the mantelpiece, 'Six shillings short, I'm afraid – it was all I could get for my propelling pencil.' He is uncovered in a deception. As one indignant official of a psychic society says, 'The facial features shown in what he said was an astral projection of the late Lord Birkenhead turned out to be those of a well-known professional footballer.'

2. Mediums attempting to manifest the spirits of the famous were always on dangerous ground. The comedian

Michael Bentine, the veteran of many séances, once noted that a sure sign of a fraudulent medium was that they would conjure up Napoleon – who would then insist on speaking English. Bentine remained a believer, however, and in his psychic autobiography, *The Door Marked Summer* (1981), he satirises the sitters rather than the medium...

Medium: [of the spirit that has been contacted] He says that he was your stepfather by your mother's third marriage – and that her maiden name was Miranda Delgado.

Sitter (grudgingly): Mm! What else does this so-called entity say?

Medium (getting annoyed): He's telling me that your younger brother's name is Aloysius Lawrence, and that he was named after your maternal grandfather, who was a well-known amateur astronomer and an acknowledged authority on asteroids.

Sitter: Can he be more specific?

Medium (exasperated): Yes! He says that he was lost at sea on the Titanic and that he left you his collection of butterflies and rare sea shells. He also says you had a dog called Bonaparte, a cat named Hildegarde and a West African parakeet that could whistle 'Ave Maria'.

Sitter: In what key?

3. From Nigel Williams's novel, *They Came From SW19* (1992)...

'They always have their séances in the back parlour – a small, drab room looking out over the back garden. It was here, a couple of years ago, that Mrs Quigley talked to my Gran. Never has there been such a low-level conversation across the Great Divide.

'Are you all right, Maureen?'

'Oh yes. I'm fine.'

'Keeping well?'

'Oh yes. On the whole. Mustn't grumble. You?'

'We're fine. How are Stephen and Sarah?'

'Oh they're fine. They're all here and they're fine.'

It really was difficult to work out who was dead and who was alive.'

At the aforementioned College of Psychic Studies, the portrait of D.D. Home, greatest of spiritualists, may have pride of place but according to my guide, the administrator, 'It's all crop circles and feng shui these days.' She was a sensible, brisk woman in cardigan and pearls; she might have been a GP, or even a JP, but she spoke with affection, like a mother who says that her daughters are all into Facebook these days. She herself was a 'sensitive', as mediums are generally called today. They operate in the College behind 'Do Not Disturb' signs, in small consultation rooms decorated with flowers and (*slightly* alarmingly) boxes of tissues. The 'sensitive' raises her vibrations and sees what comes in. There might be a message from some late friend of the client that suggests the possibility of survival, or, more usually, some less specific form of consolation couched in the language of therapy.

Mediumship, I was told, has moved 'from the particular to the general', much to the relief, presumably, of the mediums. The bar has been set lower; there is no longer the requirement of raising ghosts. But in the basement of the College are stored the photographs from the heroic, high-Victorian days, each one a reproach to the waffly modern business. In the photographs, the medium sits slumped, exhausted having given birth to the pillar of light or floating upper half of a human form, or ectoplasmic extrusion.

'Amazing aren't they?' said the administrator, rather distractedly. 'But the thing is,' she went on, as I continued leafing through the ghosts, 'that these manifestations would often take hours to appear, and with everyone rushing around these days, people just haven't got time to sit down and do it.' Her implication was that people can't be bothered to raise the dead anymore; that they have other, more important things to do than disproving the known laws of the universe.

THE SOCIETY FOR PSYCHICAL RESEARCH

For more than a hundred years, the Society for Psychical Research (the SPR) has attempted to bring 'disciplined experimental methods and standardised methods of description' to psychical research, and its members have sometimes seemed more sceptical than the sceptics.

After contacting the Society, I received an email from

one of its former Presidents, Professor Donald James West, who invited me to speak to him, before adding the proof of sanity that is obligatory in these cases: 'P.S. I am a professor of criminology and a psychiatrist'. Not that Professor West is at all boastful. In fact, the first thing he said when we met in his basement flat in Kensington (which is filled with good art and has perhaps a certain dark heaviness about it that might attest to his interests) was, 'I'm just a run of the mill academic.'

This may well not be true: he was a Professor of Clinical Criminology at Cambridge, and has written eleven books on the subject. But Professor West is comparing himself with the Olympian founders of the Society. These were three 'Trinity men' – that is, they were all sometime fellows of Trinity College, Cambridge: Henry Sidgwick, who tutored Arthur Balfour in moral philosophy at Cambridge; Frederic Myers, classical scholar, poet and originator of the terms 'telepathy' and 'sixth sense'; and Edmund Gurney, musician and psychologist. Other early Presidents included the above-mentioned Arthur Balfour, Lodge and Crookes; also Gilbert Murray (Regius Professor of Greek, and founder of the League of Nations Union after the First World War), William McDougall (Professor of Psychology at Harvard), F.J.M Stratton (Professor of Astrophysics at Cambridge), Guy William Lambert, sometime Assistant Under-Secretary of State for War. And Freud and Jung were corresponding members.

There is a slight falling off towards the modern day. The academic institutions, and positions held, are not so august, but if you fill in the on-line membership application form, the first options given under 'title' are still 'Dr' and 'Prof'.

At first, the Society engaged with spiritualism, and studied the accounts of the investigation of D.D. Home by Crookes, which had occurred before its foundation. It also monitored its own, trusted mediums, and exposed obviously fraudulent ones. But the first landmark was the publication, in 1886, of a two-volume study called *Phantasms of The Living*, which is commonly cited as the classic of psychical research. It was mainly written by Edmund Gurney, was overseen intellectually by Frederic Myers and was based on research conducted by a man called Frank Podmore. There will be more on this truly haunting book later, but for now I will mention that it was concerned with what were regarded as telepathically generated 'crisis apparitions' or 'death wraiths', such as the kind seen by my grandmother: visions of people who were at the time dying, usually many miles away from the seer of the vision or, in the jargon, 'the percipient'.

After the First World War, the emphasis shifted to the study of phenomena not necessarily connected to death: telepathy between people in perfectly good health; clairvoyance; retrocognition (visions of the past); precognition (visions of the future); false memory syndrome; and parapsychology in general. The actual ghost-trail had gone cold, and the eclipse of spiritualism and a series of internal disputes accounted for a steep drop in membership during the inter-war years.

The Society still sent out its 'investigators' – bright young men from the Universities – to the scenes of sightings, but now apparently rather tardily. In 1931 a chimney sweep called Mr Bull, of Ramsbury in Wiltshire, had died of cancer. He reappeared in his house, and was seen many times by various members of his family and their friends, since he would linger for hours on end. The family called in the vicar, who in turn wrote to the SPR asking them to come and investigate, and urging them to hurry up, since the Bulls would soon be moving into a council flat. The SPR replied with a questionnaire. The vicar filled it out and returned it, whereupon – well, after five more days – the SPR sent two investigators: Gerald Balfour, brother of Arthur, and a barrister called J.D. Piddington. When they arrived in Ramsbury, the pair found the family in the process of moving, and Mr Bull did not subsequently reappear, either in the house or the new flat.

People still ask the Society to investigate phenomena, but, Professor West told me while serving coffee and dark chocolate biscuits in his flat, 'not as much as before'.

Professor West's own psychic researches began when he was a student at Liverpool University. He was particularly interested in the work of J.B. Rhine, the American parapsychology pioneer and, taking his cue from Rhine, he 'tried to produce Extra-Sensory Perception effects under controlled conditions'. It was done by post: a matter of finding out whether people could tell what time was shown on clock cards held by Professor West. He had a dozen 'subjects'. 'Did it work?' I ask, and Professor West smiles ruefully, 'I had some interesting results with a retired engineer.' But the matter couldn't be pushed to a definitive conclusion.

Professor West's whole demeanour is wry, gently melancholic, and this I suspect of the tone of the current-day SPR as a whole. Membership is holding steady, but, at nine hundred, well down on the peak of fifteen hundred. In spite of the shift towards parapsychology, proof of survival of death remains the Holy Grail for Society members. 'But it's almost inconceivable,' says Professor West sipping his coffee, '...almost.'

Has he ever seen a ghost, I wonder?

'No,' he says, smiling, half apologetic.

After speaking to Professor West, I cycled the short distance from his flat to the headquarters of the SPR.

These are located above 'J.H. Kenyon Limited, Funeral Directors', and if that weren't Ealing Comedy-ish enough, it is not quite clear which bell push belongs to which concern. (This must be doubly annoying, since it's the business of each to put the other out of business). But I guess right, and I am admitted to the SPR rooms, the biggest of which is a library. Here, the orderly shelves, the sedate potted palms, the gentility of the two members superintending contrasts with the extravagance of the book titles: *Borderland of Psychical Research*, *Almanac of the Uncanny*, *Heavenly Lights*, *The Other Side of Death*, *Ecstasy*, *Human Personality and its Survival of Bodily Death*. On the top of one bookcase is something resembling an old-fashioned radio. The librarian tells me that nobody knows what this relic of the heroic days is, but that it is thought to be 'a machine for testing mediums'. There is a switch marked 'sensitivity', graded from 1/50, via 1/20 and ¾ to 'FULL'. Another switch gives two options: 'Galvo Lamp On' and 'Galvo Lamp Off'. Accessories in the form of two very sharp pencils and a test tube with a stopper are clipped into place on the front of the contraption.

One is always looking for some psychic event to occur in conjunction with the SPR and, sitting down in the library in order to flip through the membership directory, I see the name and address of a man who lives two doors away from me.

As I leave with a couple of books under my arm, I reflect that the strangeness of the library comes from the fact that it represents an attempt to codify the numinous. And this prompts the thought that the many libraries in ghost stories are depicted as places where the supernatural and the rational clash. As such they are dangerous, combustible places...

GHOSTS AND LIBRARIES

The ghost story character quietly reading in his library is asking for trouble. The library represents everything the ghost is against: tranquillity, normality, sceptimistm, the pursuit of the rational, and so libraries are the most important rooms in ghost stories.

In Edith Wharton's ghost story, 'Afterward' (1910), the library is the 'pivotal' feature of the Tudor house called

Lyng in Dorsetshire that the American couple are so keen to occupy, even though they have been warned it is haunted. For this Anglophile pair, Mary and Ned Boyne, the ghost is part of the attraction, along with the remoteness, the lack of electric light, hot water-pipes and 'other vulgar necessities'. They move into the house, and Ned Boyne begins work, in the library, on his book with the title – highly provocative to any spirit – *The Economic Basis of Culture*. It is while 'waiting in the library for the lamps to come' that Mary Boyle has her first misgivings about the house: 'The room itself might have been full of secrets. They seemed to be piling themselves up, as evening fell, like the layers and layers of velvet shadow dropping from the low ceiling, the rows of books, the smoke-blurred sculpture of the hearth.' And it is in the library that her husband will encounter the ghost.

The M.R. James stories feature so many academics wrongly assuming they are safe in libraries that it would be tiresome to count them. 'The Tractate Middoth' stands out as a ghost story almost entirely set in a library. Towards the end of an autumn afternoon, a thin-faced man with grey 'Piccadilly weepers' (mutton-chop whiskers) enters the library vestibule and presents to the library assistant a slip on which is written the book he wants to see. The assistant, a Mr Garrett (he's working class, of course, with a name like that) looks up the book in the index, and observes: 'Talmud: Tractate Middoth, with the commentary of Nachmanides, Amsterdam, 1707. 11.3.34. Hebrew class, of course. Not a very difficult job this.'

He's wrong about that, actually. It seems this is a popular title, and when Mr Garrett goes to find the book, he sees it being taken off the shelf by 'a shortish old gentleman, perhaps a clergyman, in a cloak', but then again the light in the library is poor at that time of day...

Libraries – or at least rooms in which people read – also occur commonly in true ghost stories.

In 1939 a book was published called *Apparitions and Haunted Houses*. It was compiled by Sir Ernest Bennett, a man described slightly disturbingly on the first page as 'Late Fellow of Hertford College, Oxford'. The book is a compendium of very plausible ghost sightings, beautifully written, and sent in by middle class percipients. The tone is melancholic and genteel. An extra man is observed by a several guests at a 'tea and music' house party. He looked a 'legal type', and was observed to do nothing more alarming than sit on the sofa reading newspapers. But who was he? Four guests asked the hostess, who absolutely denied that he had been present.

Many entries include lines like, 'After I had spent the afternoon, writing letters and reading...' 'I looked up from my book....' 'I returned to my reading...' 'I was smoking a cigarette and reading...' There is the customary praise for the 'intellectual quality' and 'soundness of mind' of the percipients, and their bookishness seems to back this up. It struck me, reading this book, that people are much more likely to see ghosts when they are alone, still, quiet, and in the semi-dream state that reading or writing can bring on. This is why ghosts and libraries go together, and why fewer ghosts are seen today.

*

It is in the context of libraries that I want to grapple with the burly, garrulous figure of Harry Price. Price styled himself 'a psychic detective' and he became famous for investigating, in the 1930's, what he called *The Most Haunted House in England*, namely Borley Rectory in Essex. The phrase was not, apparently his own. It had been suggested to him by a tourist, because Borley was the talk of Britain in the late Twenties and early Thirties. But the phrase served Price's gift for publicity, and provided the title for the first of his two books on Borley Rectory.

Price was a psychic researcher who sought intellectual respectability for the pursuit – and fame for himself. He was also, rather awkwardly as far as that first aim was concerned, a magician, a fact he does not mention in 'The Most Haunted House in England', which appeared in 1940.

The story of Borley Rectory was told me by my father when I was a young boy. I was fascinated by the baleful name of the place, and would ask him to repeat the stories, even though I knew they would keep me awake. Borley was *the* haunting of my father's formative years, and he had read about as a boy, when had had taken Price's book out of York Library. In brief, the story is as follows...

Borley Rectory was built in 1863 in order to accommodate the Reverend H.D.E Bull. It looked like a cluster of Gothic churches, and is always described as horribly ugly in the many books that have been written about it. It had, of course, a library, to which we will return.

Right from the start, the Reverend Mr Bull and his family reported ghosts – spirits of the old school, you might say: a nun walking in the gardens, a spectral coach and horses, and they weren't too bothered by them. The Reverend Mr Bull died in 1892 and his son, Harry Bull, also a reverend, took over the property with his own family. Further sightings were reported by the family, again in casual terms. I like the sound of Harry Bull. He said that he intended to return to haunt the house himself, and that he would develop a signature style of haunting 'such as throwing moth-balls about, that's it. Moth-balls, then you'll know it's me.' But one should never give such a hostage to fortune in the world of ghostliness, and after his death in 1927, moth-balls were reported as flying about the house, along with a good deal else.

The next tenants, the Reverend Mr and Mrs Eric Smith, reported poltergeist activity. Poltergeist is from the German, combining 'poltern' – to rattle – with 'geist' – meaning spirit, and we will hear more from them in Part Three. The Smiths reported stones thrown at windows, elusive footsteps, tappings and rappings, and Harry Price came to investigate in 1929. He held a séance in the garden, in which he said he'd contacted the Reverend Harry Bull.

Then the Reverend L.A. Foyster and his wife Marianne took over the place, and during their five-year tenancy the poltergeist activity became more violent. For example, Mrs

Foyster reported being nearly smothered by her own mat-
tress. Mrs Foyster was, perhaps, emotionally disturbed.
She disliked Borley Rectory; she was much younger than
her husband, and she was carrying on an affair with the
lodger in the house. Sceptics would say she invented phenomena out of hysteria. Believers would say that poltergeists derive their energy from highly charged emotional
states.

The Foysters summoned Price back to the house, so he
packed his 'ghost-hunter's kit' including 'portable telephone for communicating with an assistant in another
part of building or garden', 'note book', 'red, blue and
black pencils', 'bowl of mercury for detecting tremors in a
room', 'soft felt overshoes used for creeping, unheard
about the house in order that neither human beings nor
paranormal "entities" shall be disturbed when producing
"phenomena"', and 'flask of brandy in case member of
investigating staff or resident is injured or faints.'

The felt shoes and the brandy, I feel, are telling. Price
inhabited an Agatha Christie world of slightly rackety
gentility: of personal secretaries, cigarette cases, wain-
scoted rooms, vicars, retired Majors. A characteristic sentence from his book would be: 'I was sitting in my office in
Kensington when two ladies were announced'. He tends
to give, and receive, accounts of ghosts over lunch. One
séance that he attended, related to the Borley goings-on,
was held, somehow inevitably, in Streatham.

Resuming his investigations at Borley, Price noted sibilant whisperings, writings in pencil on the wall, asking

Marianne for 'mass' and 'candles'. These, Price assumed, were from the tormented spirit of the nun, apparently a refugee from a convent that had once existed nearby. She had had an affair with a monk from a monastery that had also been nearby. Price became very keen on this nun, and would later unearth what he claimed were her bones during an excavation of the basement of Borley, rather as Mrs Crippen's remains had been found in an excavation of Dr Crippen's basement.

Price wrote about Borley for the *Daily Mirror*, and soon regular coach excursions were coming from Chelmsford, Colchester and Bury St Edmunds to Borley – 'to see the ghost'. In 1937, after the Foysters had left Borley, Price took a year's lease on the place and moved in. On May 25th 1937, he placed an advert in the *Times* appealing for impartial observers: 'HAUNTED HOUSE. Responsible persons of leisure and intelligence, intrepid, critical, and unbiased, are invited to join rota of observers in a year's night and day investigation of alleged haunted house in Home Counties.'

This is a perfect encapsulation of the ghost-hunter's pursuit of intellectual respectability. Note, for instance, that Price did not advertise in the *Daily Mirror*, which had paid him very well to write about Borley.

Price described the response to his advertisement as 'phenomenal'. Having eliminated the 'cranks' he recruited 'some forty gentlemen and one or two ladies' of 'the right sort: 'varsity graduates, scientists, doctors of medicine, consulting engineers, army men on the active list, and so on...', and he has the magician's habit of stressing that he didn't know any of them personally. Price and a 'young Oxford friend' who prepared the house for the vigils decided to accommodate the observers in, guess where, the library. This would be the 'base room'. This was supposedly for practical reasons: the room was convenient for the hall, where many strange things had occurred, and directly beneath the 'blue room', in which both the Reverend Mr Bulls had died, and in which many strange things had also occurred. Its French windows gave easy access to the garden, which the ghostly nun patrolled. The room was also 'comfortable' and equipped with 'a large number of shelves which were permanently fixed to the walls'.

Well, it would do if it was a library. There weren't any books left on those shelves, but my suspicion would be that the library appealed to Price as a base of operations because it symbolised intellectualism, or at least rationality and objectivity.

He had built up his own library in Kensington, part of a set-up he called 'The National Laboratory of Psychical Research'. He wanted to merge this with the SPR library to create a sort of university of psychic research, but he kept having political disputes with the SPR. (He eventually left his collection of ghost books to London University who are now, I believe, looking to offload it).

Price can be seen speaking from his library in YouTube footage – boasting of his rare and ancient volumes, and speaking of his scientific methods. He looks a burly man, walking with a slight lurch and speaking with a slight slur – and a hint of a cockney accent – while smoking in a self-conscious fashion. Watching him, I wondered whether he was pissed. His double-breasted suit seemed...well, not loud exactly but fast. If he had been in an Agatha Christie novel, would Price have been the murderer? I prefer to think not. In 'Science and Parascience', Brian Inglis dryly observes that Price was 'not above assisting the production of physical phenomena with the help of physical force', and Inglis is not the only one to have thought so. But that's not to say that Price didn't come to believe, having gone to Borley as a sceptic – which is what he himself said occurred. Perhaps he was like the staff of the house rented by the narrator in Dickens's story, 'The Haunted House', Ikey and the Odd Girl: 'Let me do Ikey no injustice. He was afraid of the house, and believed in its being haunted; and yet he would play false on the haunting side, so surely as he got an opportunity. The Odd Girl's case was exactly similar. She went about the house in a state of real terror, and yet lied monstrously and wilfully, and invented many of the alarms she spread, and made many of the sounds we heard.'

In 'Appendix C' of *The Most Haunted House in England* Price lists, 'in non-technical language', the phenomena seen by his official observers. A cat's grave in the garden was found to be disturbed; a column of smoke was seen rising from the lawn for no apparent reason; three separate observers identified a 'cold spot' outside the blue room; objects were recorded as having shifted position in unoccupied rooms; more than one observer felt his coat pulled; a piece of rotten wood, a petrified frog, a 'strange coat' all of untraceable origin, were discovered in the house; one observer, hearing a faint click, discovered that he had been locked in the library (fortunately the key was on the inside). There were many unexplained sounds, including whisperings, footfalls, and – reported by Mr A.P. Drinkwater and friends at 1.41am on November 14th 1937 – a 'thump' from the upper rooms. This 'thump' is perilously close to a thing that goes 'bump' in the night, and indeed a sound specifically described as a 'bump' was recorded, but that was at four o'clock in the afternoon.

Most of the phenomena reported had appeared beforehand in ghost stories. In 'The Haunters and the Haunted' by Edward Bulwer-Lytton, for example, the two ghost hunters are locked by some spirit into their own observation room in the haunted house. Cold spots and unexplained noises appear in too many fictional ghost stories to mention. But then again they also appear in many other purportedly true ghost stories. It would surely be asking too much to expect all accounts of phenomena to be novel. If ghosts do exist then they will have certain characteristics which will be common to them.

Reading the accounts of Borley, I can't quite relinquish the idea that there might have been something in it all, but I find that absurdity does keep breaking out. For example, one of the Borley observers was the pugnacious and extrovert Dr C.E.M. Joad, head of the Department of Philosophy and Psychology at Birkbeck College, London.

He would go on to become famous as a panellist on the radio programme, 'The Brains Trust', in which his trade-mark was to begin his learned answers to questions from the audience: 'It depends what you mean by...', thus imply-ing that his questioner was an idiot. Joad is associated with mendacity in two ways.

On June 8th 1931, he was playing a game of doubles tennis in London. His partner was the humorist, Stephen Potter, and the two were losing badly to two younger, fitter men. One of these two served down a rocket, and Joad's hopelessly uncontrolled return volleyed into the stop-net-ting a good twelve feet beyond the base line, at which point he eyed his opponent questioningly before calling across the net: 'Kindly say clearly, please, whether the ball is in or out.' His well bred opponents, feeling their sportsmanship called into question, went to pieces and lost the game, and Potter was inspired to write *The Theory and Practice of Gamesmanship* (*The Art of Winning Games Without Actually Cheating*), the first of a series of very successful and very funny books with a similar theme. There's nothing funny about the second association of Joad and mendacity though. In early 1948 he was travelling by train from Waterloo to Exeter. Found to be without a ticket, he told the ticket collector he'd got on at Salisbury. He was con-victed of fare evasion and fined two pounds with twenty five guineas costs. His BBC contract was terminated, and his reputation ruined.

At Borley, Joad was one of the main sources for the reports of spontaneously appearing pencil marks on the walls, although he did introduce a note of scepticism by wondering not so much why the marks were made as *how*. How might a poltergeist get hold of a pencil, and always a sharp one at that? But if we are entitled to question Joad's evidence, can we dismiss the hundreds of other accounts of phenomena from Price's forty gentlemen and ladies? And all the accounts that predate and postdate them?

At the Borley-related Streatham séance already mentioned, which was held on March 27th 1937, a spirit called 'Sunex Amures' – a somehow very convincing name thrown up by the movement of the planchette – announced that Borley Rectory would burn down at nine o'clock that night. He, or it, was out by eleven months. The house burnt down in February 1939. Its last owner, a Captain Gregson, said he had accidentally knocked an oil lamp onto a pile of books, but the insurance company believed the fire had been started deliberately. Nine years later, Harry Price died.

But these events were not necessarily the end of either Price or the Borley ghosts, which are said to have moved their operations to Borley Church. (Even so, the residents of the house whose garden incorporates the Borley site are sick of answering the door to ghost hunters).

As for Price, according to *The Encyclopaedia of Ghosts* by Daniel Cohen (1999), a young man called Erson awoke in Sweden one night in 1948, shortly after Price's death (no closer particulars are given) to find a besuited, slightly balding man by his bed. This figure spoke English, which

Erson did not. But the figure did get across that his name was Price. He revisited Erson several times, and urged him to go and see a certain doctor. This doctor, it turned out, had an interest in psychical research and, on being told of the apparition, he explained to Erson all about the man who put Borley Rectory on the map.

MY OWN LIBRARY GHOST

The London Library is in St James's Square, London W1. It is the largest private library in the world, and it has a very good atmosphere (see the next chapter). The staircase and the main reading room have the plush cosiness of a gentleman's club, and this contrasts with the dusty bleakness of the labyrinthine book stacks. I like to work at the small desks set inside the stacks because there is always at least one person in the *communal* work spaces who constantly sniffs. On one level of the stacks there are four little desks in a row, all squeezed into the margin of an area containing English and French Literary criticism. Readers at these desks all face the same direction, like passengers on a bus.

The front desk was free, and I sat down at it. At the one behind sat a tousle-haired, public schoolboy-type with an expensive laptop, a mobile phone and an ipod on his desk. I should think he was called... Anthony. The desk behind him was empty, and at the desk behind that – the final one – sat an elderly, dusty looking man with a small, pale head, and white hair that stuck up as though he'd had an electric shock. He was looking down at a thick book and did not seem to register my arrival, or the irritatingness of Anthony, who typed noisily and kept checking his mobile for text messages before slinging it back down.

Towards one o'clock, Anthony got up, and with a lot of clattering of his belongings and scraping of his chair on the floor, cleared off, presumably to lunch. I turned around and looked directly at the man at the rear desk. As I did so, he lifted up his head.

The face, thus revealed, was even whiter than his hair, and his eyes were of an extraordinarily pale blue, like the eyes of a Siamese cat. He looked both young and old because, although his face was extraordinarily white, it was completely unlined. I was shaken by his appearance, and put off my work, so I left to go to lunch myself about five minutes later.

When I returned, Anthony was back at his desk, and the pale man was still sitting reading. Anthony left for good at about four o'clock, with more scraping and clattering. When he'd gone, I turned around. The pale man was still there, still reading. As I looked on, he slowly began to lift his head, and I turned back around quickly. Ten minutes later, I risked another look, and he wasn't there. It would have been almost impossible for him to leave his place without my hearing, especially since my thoughts had been entirely fixed on him for most of the afternoon. But I'd heard nothing.

The book he'd been reading remained on the desk. I walked over and picked it up. It was *The Registers of the*

Protestant Church at Caen (Normandy), Volume 1, edited by C.E. Hart, and published in 1907... which was just about right, I thought.

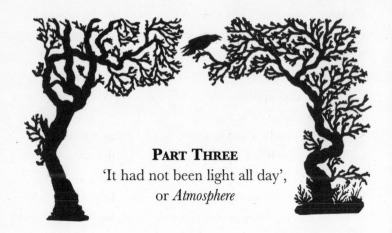

No genre is more dependent upon atmosphere than the ghost story, although it is run close in this respect by Gothic literature, which is its direct forerunner.

The most widely-read Gothic novel in modern Britain is a parody: *Northanger Abbey* by Jane Austen. The heroine, the perfectly pleasant Catherine Morland, is addicted to 'horrid' novels. Modern readers have assumed that the titles of some of the ones that excited her – *Castle of Wolfenbach*, *Mysterious Warnings*, *Necromancer of the Black Forest* etc – were made up by Austen, but these are all real books. Gothic novels might feature ghosts among a long cast list of villains both supernatural and mortal, but they were devoted to the violent and the macabre rather than to ghostliness.

I personally think of the difference between gothic fiction and ghost fiction as encapsulated by two experiences I had while in the bath.

When I was a boy, I once slipped when climbing into the bath, and sliced the side of my hand against my father's razor. I didn't notice I'd done this until I saw a red cloud unrolling within the hot water. I was transfixed by the sight, and actually put off panicking for a moment while I savoured its beauty.

More recently – about a year ago – I was sitting in the bath in the 1940's terraced house in Southwold, Suffolk that we had rented for the summer. It was late at night; I was alone in this house; the street beyond was, as usual, silent to the point of being disturbing, and I was bathing in the dark, since the bulb had gone, and I could not unscrew the glass globe that enclosed it. When I turned off the bath taps I heard a great juddering of the plumbing, which then gave way to what sounded like a babble of hoarse, indistinct voices. It must be some peculiarity of the old-fashioned plumbing system, I thought – air trapped in the pipes. (See '**Six Attempts at Putting On a Brave Face**' in Part Three). I made sure that the taps were turned fully off and waited for the noise to subside, which it didn't.

Instead, the volume increased, and distinct, sibilant words in odd conjunctions – such as 'necessary separation' – seemed to leap out. I climbed out of the bath, walked to my bedroom, and turned on Radio Five, which as usual – and thank God – was broadcasting some thoroughly inconsequential time-killing football chat. I stood there dripping and listening to it, and by the time I walked back to the bathroom I was completely dry and the noise had stopped.

Gothic literature was an offshoot of Gothic Revival architecture. Horace Walpole built the Gothic mansion, Strawberry Hill, at Twickenham in London, and also wrote *The Castle of Otranto* (1764), which is taken to be the first Gothic novel. The Gothic was a reaction against the placidity of the dominant neo-classical taste. Its adherents liked to imagine the jagged ruins of medieval abbeys or castles offset against a lowering sky. Gothic novels also belong within Romantic literature in their emphasis on place, and from these twin roots we get ghost story atmosphere, of which the primary ingredient is weather.

Michael Frayn once wrote a funny piece in the *Guardian* about the use of weather in fiction: 'The weather – that's what I want to write about. What immensely evocative stuff the weather is! Whenever I look out of the window and observe the meteorological condition of the day I can feel the grand periods pulsing in the blood, the nostalgic phrases ringing in my head. Whenever I look at the typewriter and see a blank piece of paper, the thin Atlantic cloud-wrack starts to scud across it immediately.'

Ghost story writers lay on plenty of weather, and it is seldom seen to improve when the ghost is in the offing. Rather, it *takes a turn for the worse*:

GOOD BAD WEATHER: SIX INSTANCES

1. 'The fog and frost so hung about the black old gateway of the house that it seemed as if the Genius of the Weather sat in mournful meditation on the threshold.' On Christmas Eve Scrooge approaches his house and its waiting ghosts in *A Christmas Carol* (1843) by Charles Dickens. Or see, from 'To Be Taken with a Grain of Salt' by the same author: 'I took my seat in the place appropriated to Jurors in waiting, and I looked about the Court as well as I could through the cloud of fog and breath that was heavy in it. I noticed the black vapour hanging like a murky curtain outside the great windows, and I noticed the stifled sound of wheels on the straw or tan that was littered in the street; also the hum of the people gathered there, which a shrill whistle, or, a louder song or hail than the rest, occasionally pierced.'

2. 'The lamp in the bathroom threw the most absurd shadows into the room, and the wind was beginning to talk nonsense.' From *My Own True Ghost Story* (1888) by Rudyard Kipling.

3. 'Shortly before ten o'clock the stillness of the air grew quite oppressive, and the silence was so marked that the bleating of a sheep inland or the barking of a dog in the town was distinctly heard, and the band on the pier, with its lively French air, was like a discord in the harmony of nature's silence. A little after midnight came a strange sound from over the sea, and high overhead the air began to carry a strange, faint, hollow booming.' From *Dracula* (1896) by Bram Stoker, preceding the arrival of the Count at Whitby. This is more of a Gothic novel than a ghost story, admittedly, but Stoker is something of a weather specialist. In 'Dracula's Guest', a short story originally intended for inclusion in the novel, the manifestation of the demons in the countryside near Munich on Walpurgis Night is preceded by the narrator experiencing first a fleeting breath of cold wind on an otherwise sunny evening; dark clouds begin to muster overhead; the wind rises and the air turns icy cold. There is then both thunder and lightning and snow and – bit later on – a tornado.

4. Ghost story writers are so keen on weather that they sometimes like to get two descriptions of it in for the price of one. In 'All Hallows' (1942) by Walter de le Mare, the narrator arrives at the apparently deserted, remote cathedral on the edge of the sea. It is a hot August afternoon. The great cathedral is 'lulled as if into a dream by this serenity of air and heavens'. The narrator then wonders 'what kind of first showing it would have made...if an autumnal gale had been shrilling and trumpeting across its narrow bay – clots of wind-borne spume floating among the dusky pinnacles – and the roar of the sea echoing against its walls. Imagine it frozen stark in winter, icy hoarfrost edging its every boss, moulding, finial, crocket, cusp!' Or here is an interpolation in M.R. James's story, 'A View From a Hill' (1925): 'Writing as I am now with a winter wind flapping against dark windows and a rushing, tumbling sea within a hundred yards, I find it hard to summon up the feelings and words which will put my reader in possession of the June evening and the lovely English landscape of which the Squire was speaking.'

5. 'It was a lovely July evening, and the air was delicate with the scent of the pine-woods...As they entered the avenue of Canterville Chase, however, the sky became suddenly overcast with clouds, a curious stillness seemed to hold the atmosphere, a great flight of rooks passed silently over their heads and, before they reached the house, some big drops of rain had fallen.' From 'The Canterville Ghost' (1887) by Oscar Wilde.

6. 'Sounds were deadened, shapes blurred. It was a fog that had come three days before, and did not seem inclined to go away and it had, I suppose, the quality of all such fogs – it was menacing and sinister, disguising the familiar world and confusing the people in it, as they were confused by having their eyes covered and being turned about, in the game of Blind Man's Buff.' From *The Woman in Black* (1983) by Susan Hill. There are about three pages on this fog, which sets the scene for the start of the ghost story proper in chapter two. Susan Hill is very strong on atmosphere. She once wrote an account, in *The Spectator*, of a long, hot day in the country (culminating in a bee sting) that practically gave me sunstroke. She is a disciple of the master, and I recall reading another piece, about her plans for Christmas, in which she wrote: 'This Christmas's Dickens is *Pickwick Papers*.'

*

From a leisure pursuits point of view, ghostliness is one

of the few things that British weather is good for. Ghostliness generally is a north European attribute. As Peter Davidson writes in *The Idea of North*, 'Ghosts are less a feature of southern belief than are beliefs in vampires and the evil eye – both of which are direct inheritances from the Romans... But the revenant narrative is essentially of the north, and is a product of occluded weather and broodings on the fate of the dead.' Since there is even more weather in Scotland than in England, there is even more ghostliness there too, which is why every castle in Scotland has its attendant ghosts. And the winter days are shorter there, which also helps...

DARKNESS

Darkness is the other essential element of ghostliness.

Most of us are immune from total darkness, in that we seldom walk down a country road on a moonless night without a torch. Try it, and you will see a ghost, I guarantee. I once went on an 'investigation' (I thought of it as a 'ghost hunt' but I knew the term was disapproved of) with a ghost club based at...well, I'd better just say a town in the Midlands. It was a late spring evening, and before proceeding to the haunted location – a country house just outside the town – we sat around in one of the member's houses for a couple of hours. Ostensibly we were being briefed; the packed lunches were being handed out and the contents verified; the vehicle – it was always 'the vehicle' and never the 'car' – that would take us to the house was being loaded. But I believed that the real purpose of the delay was to wait for darkness to fall. And when we arrived at the haunted house, there was a great fetishisation of torches. The leader of the club naturally had the biggest one; but we were all equipped with two, and there was a reserve of spare batteries. As in the 'Famous Five' stories of Enid Blyton, torches, packed lunches and maps were all very important, but the torches especially. The torches gave light but, more to the point, they gave darkness when turned off. At certain times, certain members of the party would be sent to patrol the grounds of the house with torches switched off. I myself completed two circuits of the grounds, at about 2am and 4am. On both occasions the two men I was with – seasoned ghost hunters – reported back that nothing had been seen. I kept quiet, but on both occasions I personally saw dozens of ghosts, or what might easily have *been* ghosts: blurred shapes moving low over the lawn; things skimming across the surface of the ornamental lake; bushes rustling and moving unaccountably.

I put all this down to the activity of birds. I had been taught that birds roosted at night, but I told myself that they can't all be roosting all the time. Perhaps they spent a good deal of time moving – silently and ultra-fast – from one roosting position to another. But the real cause of my visions was the darkness.

We have seen that medieval life was a veritable phantasmagoria, and no wonder given the lack of street lights or, indeed, streets. A walk in the dark at night would set anyone back about five hundred years. The Enlightenment, which brought the banishment of ghosts from everyday life, must in part have been a literal enlightening: the proper lighting of domestic and public spaces was not far behind, after all. We have seen that the Victorian Spiritualists preferred a reversion to low light, whether because the spirits preferred it, or for less creditable reasons – and it is said that infra-red photography (photography that can see in the dark) was the final knell for physical mediumship. But in his above-mentioned book, *The Door Marked Summer* (1981), the comedian Michael Bentine, provides a rationale for darkness in séances – a rationale that seems to become more disturbing with each successive word:

'Darkness is mandatory for physical phenomena and it does make sense. Firstly, the darkness precludes the possibility of the attention of the sitters being drawn to the objects that, even in a bare room, catch the eye. Secondly, if, as we believed, the generation of the coarser form of ectoplasm required to contain and sustain a tangible field of force sufficient to levitate a human being is ultra-sensitive to light then, obviously, the absence of light becomes necessary.'
(I'm not sure that word 'obviously' is strictly justified there).

And here is a rationale for darkness in ghost stories. It comes from the female narrator of 'The Lost Stradivarius'

(1895) by John Meade Falkener. She is explaining to her nephew how his late father became susceptible to ghostliness: 'Any trouble or fear becomes, as you will some day learn, my dear nephew, immensely intensified and exaggerated at night. It is so, I suppose, because our nerves are in an excited condition, and our brain not sufficiently awake to give a due account of our foolish imaginations.'

The writer of a ghost story often has to find a means of bringing about absolute darkness. In a modern ghost story the house is an isolated property not on the mains, and the generator packs up. A practically minded man goes outside with a torch, saying, 'It just needs a kick in the right place – be back in a sec,' and that is the last we see of *him*. The neatest rationale for darkness that I can think of is in *A Christmas Carol* by Charles Dickens: 'Darkness is cheap, and Scrooge liked it.' But then it was generally much easier for a writer to snuff out the light in Victorian days because there was so little of it to start with. All that was required was a sudden gust of wind that might blow out a candle, and this was already a clichéd prelude to terror when Jane Austen wrote *Northanger Abbey*. (In the eponymous gloomy house, the heroine, Catherine Morland, is reading at night when the candle inexplicably blows out, which seems a bit over the top, since she's perusing nothing more momentous than the laundry list.)

In her book *Coal, A Human History*, Barbara Friese points out that Britain, alone in Northern Europe, preferred open fires to iron stoves for domestic heating, the point being that the open fire was also a source of low light. It was part of our taste for cosiness. We are a cosy nation. Consider Winston Churchill, who won the War from his bed, or Delia Smith, whom I nominate as the Queen of Cosy. Take this from *Delia Smith's Complete Cookery Course* (Classic Edition): 'Although you can buy good crumpets, I do think they're fun to make – especially on a cold snowy day, when everyone's housebound.' (I think she means 'snowbound', since 'housebound' suggests confinement owing to illness).

Our cosiness, and correspondingly our ghostliness, comes to the fore at Christmas, which I will now consider before moving on to its poor relation, Halloween.

CHRISTMAS

It was Dickens who, in the words if his biographer Peter Ackroyd, 'made Christmas cosy'. Before him, it was a rather pallid festival, somewhat like Easter in that, if you were distracted or very poor, you might not notice it.

Ackroyd writes that Dickens's insecure childhood gave him 'an acute sense of, and need for "Home"'. As far as Dickens was concerned, the worse things could be made to seem outside the house, the better they were in it, hence the Christmas ghost story told around the fire. For years, anyone who received a Christmas card from me (a very select group indeed) got a picture of Mr Pickwick warming his vast rear end before a fire, above a caption reading, '"This," said Mr Pickwick, looking around him, "This is, indeed, comfort.".' Mr Pickwick was depicted at Dingley

Dell (the convivial house to which the Pickwickians often repaired) just before the telling of the first of Dickens's Christmas ghost stories:

> 'Ah!' said the old lady. 'There was just such a wind, just such a fall of snow, a good many years back, I recollect – just five years before your poor father died. It was Christmas Eve, too; and I remember that on that very night, he told us the story about the Goblins that carried away old Gabriel Grub.'

This is the cue for a trial run for *A Christmas Carol* in that it is the tale of a misanthrope who apprehends the Christmas message by supernatural agencies. I watched an adaptation of *A Christmas Carol*, or read it, on almost every Christmas of my childhood, and in 1970 I went to the York Odeon to see 'Scrooge' – not the revered, unfrightening version of 1951, starring Alistair Sim, but a version made in 1970 with Albert Finney as the miser. Unaware that the film critic Leslie Halliwell had pronounced, 'Dim musical version, darkly coloured and quite lost on the wide screen...', I was haunted for years by that film. Halliwell conceded that 'It has its macabre moments of trick photography', and it was the scene where Scrooge falls towards the red hot caverns of hell that would revisit me.

Then there was Dylan Thomas's story 'A Child's Christmas In Wales', which I owned in an edition with illustrations by Edward Ardizzone, and which was read out at a school carol service, in about 1973, by my favourite English teacher, Mr Milner. (Or was it Mr Hurd, my other favourite?) As a story, it has excellent atmosphere. It only becomes ghostly – and then very effectively – towards the end.

I believe that I would say the word 'Ghost' after 'Christmas' in any word association game, but the connection pre-dates the era of the modern ghost story. As Julia Briggs writes in *Night Visitors: The Rise and Fall of the English Ghost Story*: 'In folklore, ghosts had long been connected with Christmas Eve, just as they were with several other Christian festivals, in particular Halloween... The appearance of ghosts on Christmas Eve could be explained in Christian terms as the disturbance of souls in Purgatory, before the advent of the Saviour at midnight brought them peace.'

But compare and contrast this, spoken by Horatio in *Hamlet*:

Some say, that ever 'gainst that season comes
Wherein our Saviour's birth is celebrated,
The bird of dawning singeth all night long:
And then (they say) no spirit can walk abroad,
The nights are wholesome, then no planets strike,
No fairy takes, nor witch has power to charm:
So hallow'd and so gracious is the time.

Briggs argues that this reassurance was not believed; that the proverb 'ghosts never appear on Christmas Eve' was intended ironically, a maxim for the complacent.

HALLOWEEN

For all its commercialisation our Christmas remains cosy, and to some extent ghostly, but that is more than can be said for our Halloween.

When I was a boy, Halloween was a shadowy, elusive affair: the occasional carved pumpkin glowing in a window; the occasional fleeting glimpse of a reveller skipping away in a witch's hat – usually some person you didn't know, and had never seen before. As a festival, it was upstaged by Bonfire Night, and I was frustrated by Halloween in those days. There was nothing you could buy, or be given, in connection with it. Today, there is a great deal you can buy, as a result of the promotion of Trick or Treat, by which Halloween has eclipsed Bonfire Night, and ghostliness has given way to mock horror. In the weeks before Halloween, Asda stores offer, amid a landslide of plastic tat: the Asda Squeezy Eyeball, the Asda Rat, the Asda Inflatable Coffin, the Child Grim Reaper Outfit ('One size fits all'), the Adult Grim Reaper Outfit, the Inflatable Pumpkin Cooler (not for cooling pumpkins, you understand), the Skull Martini Shaker.

Asda is American-owned, and Trick or Treat came to us from America. The British folklorist, Doc Rowe, believes the Trick or Treat contagion began with a programme broadcast on ITV in the early Seventies as part of a documentary strand called 'Look Stranger'. It depicted life on the American airbase in Woodbridge, Suffolk, and showed the children trick-or-treating. 'Within two years,' Doc Rowe told me, 'all the tabloids were running features on how to dress up for the occasion.' But his point is that this was merely the re-introduction into this country of a tradition rooted in our psychology.

It helps to think of both Halloween and Bonfire Night as outgrowths of the Celtic celebration called Samhain, which marked the turning of their year and the beginning of winter. Samhain was associated with the lighting of fires to honour the dead, and defy malevolent spirits. The medieval Church both denounced the festivals as diabolic and sought to appropriate aspects of them in the shape of All Saints Day on November 1st (on which the sanctified are honoured), and All Souls Day on November 2nd (a more democratic honouring of all Christian souls).

According to Doc Rowe, 'By tarring Halloween with an occult brush, by caricaturing it in that way, the church *made* it an occult event.' But while the original Halloween might not have been thoroughgoingly sinister, it did incorporate games and rituals of licensed naughtiness. A remnant of these is Mischief Night, which occurs in pockets of the north of England especially on November 4th. In the York of my boyhood, the jape was to remove gates from hinges, and leave them piled up on street corners. Doc Rowe brackets this tradition of naughtiness as 'misrule' or 'world-turned-upside-down' and there are elements of it even in the Christianised medieval version of Halloween. All Souls Day, for example, was associated with Soul Caking, wherein poor Christians would say prayers for the departed relations of wealthier ones in return for food – and you can see how there might have been trouble if the rich didn't play along. Similar traditions are associated with May Day. It is as though the arrival of a new season brings a shifting of the scenery, during which the leading actors are distracted, allowing the bit-part players to have their chance.

It is likely that these traditions, precursors of Trick or Treat, were taken to America by Scottish and Irish emigrants of the mid-nineteenth century... So the Asda Inflatable Coffin is actually our fault. But Doc Rowe believes these customs are ineradicable in any case: 'The more you suppress these things, the greater they become.'

Apart from the Church, he identifies the main suppressors as 'the health and safety camp'. I know what he means, and I wonder how long it will be before the words 'high visibility vest' come up in a ghost story.

ANTI-ATMOSPHERE

Our workplaces and public spaces are required to be adequately lit, and it seems there is never anyone sitting in on the planning meetings who will querulously interpose: 'Yes, I agree we must do something about all the muggings in the dark alleys near the canal, but not at the expense of the *atmosphere*, surely?'

It would be useless to complain. It's just that adequately lit usually means overlit. Take our buses. The original interior colour scheme of London's fabled double-decker, the Routemaster, featured Burgundy lining panels, Chinese green window surrounds, and Sung yellow ceilings, all illuminated with bulbs of the lowest possible wattage. 'Even fifteen years ago,' writes Travis Elborough in *The Bus We Loved*, 'to travel on a Routemaster with the remnants of its original decor intact felt like being conveyed about the city in the lounge of an illustrious, if by now gone-to-seed, club.' The Routemaster's successors have sky blue interiors and fluorescent yellow interiors. In the *Evening Standard*, Andrew Gilligan wrote that being inside them makes him feel as though he's at the bottom of a swimming pool.

A measure of gloom might once have denoted poverty. It is now only the smartest places that have subdued lighting. And only the smartest establishments have a real fire – such as Claridge's Hotel. Here is what Dickens could see in a fire: (It's from his story of 1848, 'The Haunted Man'): 'When it was just so dark, as that the forms of things were indistinct and big, but not wholly lost. When sitters by the fire began to see wild faces and figures, mountains and abysses, ambuscades and armies, in the coals.' Can you have a ghost story told around a radiator? It might be an interesting challenge to create that frame; to have the narrator beginning his story after asking for the heating to be turned up in the Community Centre, while one of his supposed listeners takes a mobile phone call and, in the background, the commercial radio station that presumptuously calls itself 'London's Heart' plays 'Money's Too Tight To Mention' by Simply Red for the fifteenth time that day.

The simplest thing is to set a ghost story in the past, so as to access the real fires, candles, rectories etc. But the usual trappings might be abandoned for two reasons: firstly for comic effect. In any ghost story collection, you can spot the one trying this by its title. In *The Virago Book of Ghost Stories* (1987), it is 'The Haunted Saucepan' by Margery Lawrence. (A woman rents a modest, modern semi and finds herself somehow mesmerised into cleaning the place). In a similar, bathetic vein is *The Celestial Omnibus* (1911) by E.M. Forster, which is about a bus that goes to heaven, although the protagonist – a nine year- old boy resident at Agathox Lodge, 28 Buckingham Park Road, Surbiton – doesn't know it. As the bus ascends, he muses, 'even if it were Richmond Hill they ought to have been at the top long ago.' Let me invent a few titles in this line: 'The Karaoke Night Ghost', 'The Haunted Mobile Phone Shop', and I would have written 'The Haunted Tesco's', except that there really is one. In *The Mammoth Book of True Hauntings* (2008) Pater Haining writes: 'The 24-hour Tesco Superstore in Bury St Edmunds, Suffolk, has been plagued by a spectre that has been haunting the store's cafeteria in the small hours...The supermarket stands near the remains of the medieval St Saviour's Hospital, traditionally home for the ghost of a "Grey Lady".'

The other reason for spurning traditional atmosphere is to boost your ghost – to show that the spirit can assert itself outside its comfort zone – and the best ghost story writers do take on modernity. Dickens addressed the disturbing development of high speed train travel in his story,

'The Signalman' (1865), of which more below. Even the antiquarian M.R. James arranged, in 'Casting the Runes', for a supernatural message to appear in the space reserved for adverts on a tram. The eponymous public house in Kingsley Amis's ghost novel, *The Green Man* (1969), is very carefully located: 'With the A595 just too far off for individual vehicles to be heard, and no-one, for the moment, moving about in the forecourt, everything seemed quiet...'

Actually the A595 is already starting to sound quaint, but some modern phenomena are ghostly from the moment they are built or invented. We saw with regard to spiritualism that this was true of wireless telegraphy. The same goes for space travel in my view. Science Fiction and ghost stories are two genres that prop each other up. There is darkness, broken by bursts of luminosity; time travel; science and cod-science; the infinite.

Mobile Phone Cameras are also ghostly. I photographed myself once, in order to review a haircut I'd just had, and when I looked at the portrait it blinked at me. I *assume* there's some rational explanation for that. CCTV is in the same category. A crime is committed, and the police proudly publish a photograph of... a *ghost*, and one just as likely to cause dissension and recrimination as those taken at the Victorian séances.

THE HAUNTED HOUSE

If ghost stories arose from the Gothic tradition, which was

as much architectural as literary, it is also the case that persistent ghosts need a persistent location in which to manifest. So no wonder houses are haunted.

Haunted houses tend to be old and big. Such properties appeal to the romantic idea of faded grandeur, and also a baser snobbery. Every account of the above-mentioned Borley Rectory, 'the most haunted house in England', describes it as hideous, but when I look at the pictures I wonder how much it would cost today if it were still standing, and whether the seller would take a low offer in view of its poltergeist infestation. Reading ghost stories we are torn: yes, a malevolent spirit stalks the east wing, but at least there's an east wing for it to stalk. Ghost stories, both real and fictional, sometimes come with floor plans of the haunted area – literally, property particulars – and very mouth-watering they usually are.

Haunted houses also come with libraries, as we have seen, and with servants. The protagonist in a ghost story is quite alone in his huge house...except for his fifteen servants. The reader might not know about the servants until one of them hesitantly knocks and enters the master's study on the final page and finds him slumped in his chair 'With such a look on his face, the like of which I've never seen...'

The author denigrates the house, but also slyly boosts it to engage our snobbery. In Walter de le Mare's story, 'Out of the Deep' (1923) the protagonist, Jimmie, inherits his uncle's 'horrible old London mansion'. But how horrible and old can a London mansion be? In 'Moonlight

Sonata' (1931) by Alexander Woollcott, one of the two principals inhabits 'the collapsing family manor house to which he had indignantly fallen heir.' The owner is down to his last gardener, who tends the 'once sumptuous' grounds, but the place doesn't sound too bad to me. For example, 'The clock tower had been contemptuously scattering the hours like coins ever since Henry VIII was a rosy stripling'. 'The Mystery of the Semi-Detached' by Edith Nesbitt (1893) seems, from its title, to be bucking the trend, but the house is 'commodious', with several sitting rooms.

I myself grew up in a semi-detached of a more modest sort. We were its first occupants, and I was proud of inhabiting a new house. Those of my contemporaries who lived in old houses seemed to me to be taking a considerable risk. They were living in houses in which people had died, and people they didn't know, at that – people that nobody currently *alive* knew. It must be like living in a tomb. There would have to be certain echoes. In grappling with the subject in his collection of sightings, 'Apparitions and Haunted Houses', Sir Ernest Bennett plaintively wonders, 'Can it conceivably be the case that in some inscrutable fashion the woodwork and masonry of a house may exert some physical or mental influences which cause certain individuals to see the phantasmal figure of a former resident?'

A friend of my friend David's is an American poet, blogger, journalist and all-round intellectual resident in London. She's called Ada – well, at least that's what I'm calling her. Being American, she is perhaps extra-sensitive to the oldness of London...

 Ada's Haunted House

'It would have been 1988 or '89. I was staying with friends in Pendrell Road, London SE4 – a late Victorian house. It got too late to go home, so it was decided I would spend the night there. There was a basement kitchen, and I was put up on a sofa in a little room behind it that had been converted into a sitting room. I went to sleep and sometime in the wee hours I woke up to see this green... shape. It was a translucent cloud, and there was something inside the outline. As I looked it resolved itself into a thin woman making a sort of pendulum motion with her arm, and there was a horrible energy to it, a horrible scary energy. It slowly became clear to me what she was doing: she was ironing. Once I'd worked this out, the green cloud grew and grew and then disappeared.'

(In a Victorian report by the SPR, the authors noted, from the hundreds of accounts of sightings they'd sifted, that 'a fading away, occasionally accompanied by an expansion of the figure' is a common way for a ghost to depart).

The older and more atmospheric the house, the more ghosts it will have. Any stately mansion open to the public needs at least one certificated ghost, just as it needs its health and safety clearances, and someone standing at the front door to collect the money. But there is a dutiful quality about these hauntings, and they are always described evasively, in the passive voice: 'It is said that...' 'Legend has it that...' They have all the magic and mystery of the following sentences from the introduction to a book called 'Stately Ghosts', published in 2007 by the Historic Houses Association: 'The interest in ghosts and supernatural phenomena of all kinds attracts a growing number of visitors to Britain's historic houses and is helping to boost the contribution they make to the wider economy. With more than 15 million visitors, providing employment for upwards of 10,000 people (who annually earn in excess of £85 million) and contributing an estimated £1.6–£2 billion each year to the rural economy, our historic houses form a vital link between past and present.'

But no book on British ghostliness can ignore the following half dozen.

1. The Tower of London

Historically, the main business of the Tower of London (which is the number one tourist attraction in the city) was the imprisoning and execution of people who didn't deserve to be either imprisoned or executed. Accordingly the Tower is practically a ghost-making factory. The most famous case is that of the Princes in the Tower, the twelve-year old Edward V and his ten-year-old brother, Richard, Duke of York. They were killed in 1483, possibly by their uncle, the Duke of Gloucester. Certainly, their deaths cleared the way for him to assume the throne as Richard III. Naturally, the Tower was said to be haunted by the Princes. In 1674, workmen found the skeletons of two boys in a wooden chest. King Charles II ordered that the skeletons be given a royal burial, which laid the ghosts, but many others took up the baton, including such former inmates as Sir Walter Raleigh, Guy Fawkes and Anne Boleyn, the second wife of Henry VIII, who was executed in the Tower. In his book, *The Encyclopaedia of Ghosts* Daniel Cohen writes, 'Anne's ghost has been spotted frequently in the Tower, both with and without her head.'

In 1800 or so, a Tower guard fainted – and was apparently permanently incapacitated by – the sight of a huge black bear standing on its hind legs, at which point I think the ghostliness of the Tower begins to become interesting. I believe that I would be permanently incapacitated by such a sight. In 'An Account of Some Strange Disturbances in Aungier Street' by Sheridan Le Fanu, the young narrator is roused from his bed by the sound of a slow, heavy tread descending the staircase (this is a house of which he is supposedly the sole occupant). He climbs out of bed, takes up his poker, and steps into the hallway, where he sees, or thinks he sees in the darkness, 'a black monster, whether in the shape of a man or a bear I could not say...' In 1817, Edmund Swifte, keeper of the Crown Jewels, was dining in his private quarters when he saw floating in mid-air, a cylinder filled with a blue, bubbling liquid – which is another good one, I think: a beautifully irrelevant apparition.

2. Hampton Court Palace, Richmond, Surrey

Hampton Court – rated by Visit London as one of the capital's top ten tourist attractions – was built for Henry VIII's henchman Thomas Wolsey, who gave it to the king in 1528, in a futile attempt to keep in with him. Henry made it the most opulent of his palaces. There is a white lady, a grey lady, and a page boy ghost, but the principals are Henry's wives: Jane Seymour (who patrols the Clock Court with a lighted candle); Catherine Howard (whose screams are heard on the anniversary of her arrest, which occurred at Hampton Court), and Anne Boleyn (who walks Hampton Court as well as the Tower of London). In the late sixteenth or early seventeenth century, a family occupying an apartment in the Tower heard a persistent rumbling noise from behind a certain wall. This was knocked down, and a spinning wheel was found – a very good pay-off.

3. Burton Agnes Hall, Burton Agnes, near Driffield, East Yorkshire

This was built for three aristocratic sisters called Griffith, who observed the completion of their fine Jacobean mansion from premises over the road. When the house was nearly finished, in about 1628, Anne Griffith was attacked by robbers. As she lay dying, she insisted her head be kept at all times within the new house – a morbid wish commonly accounted for by her death delirium, and one ignored by her family who buried her body, including the head, outside the house. Cue much banging of doors and unprovoked rearing of horses etc. The head – now a skull – was detached from the body, and placed inside the house. It is, perhaps, walled up behind a panel in one of the bedrooms. The owners know, but will not say, or at least they say they do. Even so, the ghost of Anne Griffith – fawn in colour – still walks the house, along with many tourists, since Burton Agnes Hall is open to the public. Besides the house, there's a gift shop and garden shop, an ice cream parlour, and a children's playground with guinea pigs.

4. Markyate Cell, near Dunstable, Hertfordshire

This oddly named house was constructed in 1539 on the site of a Benedictine priory called St Trinity-in-The Wood. (Monks' habitations are cells, hence the name). By the seventeenth century, it had come into the hands of a Lady Ferrers, who is supposed to have taken to highway robbery as a sort of hobby. Some of her victims were the dinner party guests of her husband, whom she hated. She would rob them, disguised in full armour, on remote stretches of Watling Street, which was adjacent to the house, and is now the A5. The legend became the subject of a Victorian ballad, and then a film in 1945 starring Margaret Lockwood as *The Wicked Lady* ('A mixture of hot passion and cold suet pudding' – *Guardian*).

She was shot during one of her ambushes and died in

the house at the foot of a staircase leading to a secret chamber where she changed back into women's clothes. After her burial, this chamber was bricked up. The house subsequently burnt down three times, the last fire occurring in 1840. A gang of locals who were putting out the fire on behalf of the owner, a Mr Adey, saw the Wicked Lady swinging Tarzan-like on the branch of a tree – a compelling detail, I think. This haunting is in all the topographical guides to British ghosts, probably because of Margaret Lockwood. The present owner of what is now called Cell Park, Valerie Carr, was recently quoted in the *Daily Telegraph* as saying that the part of the house containing the bricked up chamber 'felt strange when we first arrived – it is certainly colder than the rest of the house.'

5. Littlecote House, Hungerford, Berkshire

A very magnificent example of Tudor architecture, according to Peter Underwood in his 'A-Z of British Ghosts' (1971). He commends the hand painted Chinese wallpaper in the drawing room, the unusual egg-shaped library, the Dutch Parlour, the Cromwellian chapel and 'the several ghosts'. The main one is that of Sir William Darrell who, in 1575 or so, had impregnated a servant. When she went into labour, he sent for a midwife, but arranged for her to be brought to the house blindfolded. The reason for this became evident when the baby was delivered: he flung it on the fire. The midwife was then paid handsomely and sent away, again blindfolded. But she deduced the location of the house from the time she had spent in the carriage etc, and Darrell was prosecuted, only for his eminence to earn him a nolle prosequi. (The trial was abandoned, in other words).

The story is supported by a fragment of a letter, dated January 2nd 1566, and discovered in 1879 in the archive of the neighbouring mansion, Longleat. It was addressed to Sir John Thynne, the owner of Longleat, and requested him to ask a tenant of his, brother of a mistress of Darrell's, questions concerning the children sired by Darrell: 'how many there were and what became of them'... which all sounds very like the beginning of a ghost story by M.R. James or one of the other antiquarians, and these events *are* treated fictionally in Sir Walter Scott's novel, *Rokeby*, in which Sir William Darrell becomes 'Wild Will'.

But as to the real ghosts...

In 1598, Darrell fell off his horse by a spot called 'Darrell's style'. The theory is that either he or the horse (or perhaps both) was startled by the sight of a flaming baby. Darrell haunts that spot, and a certain room in the house, the floor of which, according to Christina Hole *Haunted England* (1940), 'can never be kept in repair but constantly moulders away'. He has also been blamed for phantom hounds, a phantom coach, and screams coming from the landing where the murder occurred. In *The A-Z of British Ghosts*, Peter Underwood recounts that in 1927, Sir Edward Wills, of the tobacco family, which had recently taken over the house, saw a female ghost holding a light 'in the passage beyond the Long Gallery'. Sir Edward described her poignantly: 'Her hair was fair, she was not very tall...' She walked into the bedroom of Sir Edward's younger brother. He observed that she opened the door herself, which was promising. But the younger brother slept on, and the ghost disappeared.

Littlecote House is today Littlecote House Hotel, run by Warner Leisure Hotels ('Exclusively for adults'). No mention is made of Wild Will in the hotel website, but it is stressed at the foot of the homepage that 'Littlecote House is a non-smoking hotel.'

6. Glamis Castle, Angus, Scotland

Glamis is the most haunted Castle in Scotland, which is saying something. It is name-checked in Macbeth, and is taken to be the site of the murder of King Duncan, but it was not the venue for the appearance of the actual ghost in the play: that of Banquo. Today, Glamis is the residence of the eighteenth Earl of Strathmore, and, less romantically, a 'Visitor Attraction', which sounds tautological. It hosts corporate events, and is open to the public. Visitors are shown the room in which King Duncan was killed, and told about Malcolm II of Scotland, who is also said to have been murdered at Glamis, in a room that was sealed up because the bloodstains on the floor could never be removed. (In Oscar Wilde's parody ghost story, 'The Canterville Ghost', the breezy American owner of an English country house applies 'Pinkerton's Champion Stain Remover and Paragon Detergent' to a similarly obstinate bloodstain). In *The Encyclopedia of Ghosts* (1999), Daniel Cohen ruefully observes, 'How an eleventh-century murder could have taken place in a castle that was not built until the fourteenth century it is impossible to say.' There is, anyhow, supposed to be an elusive room at Glamis, and Cohen tells of how it used to be customary to hang towels from every room in the castle, but when this display was viewed from the grounds there was one window at which no towel could be seen, and every attempt to locate this window from inside the castle proved fruitless.

In the eighteenth century, the legend grew that each successive Earl of Strathmore was briefed about the contents of the room by the steward of the castle on reaching the age of maturity, whereupon they immediately became much more gloomy and introspective, and remained so for life. By the late nineteenth century, they had stopped wanting to know.

Another Glamis story concerns the second Earl, a drunken lout who was always stuck for someone to drink and play cards with and generally swear at on the Sabbath. One Sunday a black-clad figure turned up at the door offering a game in which the Earl, having run out of money, threw his soul into the pot. He lost, as does anyone who stakes their soul, as far as I'm aware.

I telephoned Glamis and asked a receptionist about ghostliness at the castle, whereupon she immediately had a coughing fit, which was intriguing. But when, still spluttering, she passed me over to her colleague, I was told,

'Nothing has been seen recently. Is there anything else I can help you with?'

THE AVOIDED HOUSE

But I am more interested in what Dickens called *avoided* houses. In any street of any length, there's one of these: a vacant house, or one that changes hands too often, or not often enough; a house in shadow, or one being taken over by its own garden. There were a couple of these on my paper-round when I was a boy. One had cracked windows, and a decaying Transit van parked immediately in front of the front door. Another had the curtains permanently closed and a front garden filled with rubble. I was encouraged by this rubble. I thought: 'One day soon they're going to use it to construct something marvellous like a pond with a fountain.' But the rubble just remained. I never saw the occupants of either house, and I didn't want to. I found it hard to imagine them going into Ellis's newsagents and paying for the newspapers I delivered to them. That would require a degree of normality incompatible with the state of their homes. I monitored, and avoided, several of this type of house in my particular suburb of York, and if I heard that a divorce or death had occurred in one of them I was secretly gratified. My stigmatisation was justified. Nothing could be done for those houses, a fact to which their owners were presumably resigned, and, by the way, I love the fatalism of the landlord of the haunted house in the above-mentioned story,

'The Haunters and the Haunted' by Edward Bulwer-Lytton (1859): 'I spent some money in repainting and roofing it, added to its old-fashioned furniture a few modern articles, advertised it, and obtained a lodger for a year. He was a colonel retired on half pay. He came in with his family, a son and a daughter, and four or five servants; they all left the house the next day...'

It didn't take much for me to condemn a property; it didn't have to be semi-derelict. For example, I wasn't very keen on any of the houses facing our own because they didn't have the sun on them in the morning; and some of my friends' houses just felt wrong inside. I am not going to broach the subject of psycho-geography because I find myself dying with exhaustion at the typing of the word, but it has been argued that houses with a reputation for being haunted occupy sites where ley lines intersect. Also blamed – and I like this – is carbon monoxide poisoning. This occurs where carbon combustion occurs with too little ventilation, and there's quite a neat fit with ghostliness in that the symptoms can include anxiety and hallucinations. People burning wood or coal, or using coal-gas lighting in a shuttered room might be at risk, which connects the condition with Victorian winters – a fertile time for ghost stories.

When I first came to London I was amazed at the number of avoided houses. They constituted about fifteen per cent of the total stock. Even the most respectable streets had them and indeed the best-known avoided house in London is in one of its grandest squares.

In his book, *London Lore: The Legends and Traditions of the World's Most Vibrant City*, Steve Roud identifies the legends surrounding the Georgian house at 50 Berkeley Square as offering a scenario that 'fits perfectly with how folklore works'.

The property had stood vacant and uncared for in the 1850's and 1860's, an affront to the elegance of the Square. It began to be talked about in society drawing rooms. In the early 1870's there was correspondence about it in the journal, 'Notes and Queries'. Lord Lyttelton wrote: 'There are strange stories about it [the house], into which this deponent can't enter.' In December 1880 a letter was published in the journal recounting a story told to the correspondent by a 'Mrs---', who had heard it from a 'Miss H---'. It told of a certain room in the upper reaches of number 50, which was being prepared for a guest by a maid working late. At the stroke of midnight, a piercing scream was heard from the room. Members of the household rushed upstairs to find the maid having convulsions at the foot of the stairs, and staring fixedly at a certain corner of the ceiling. She was taken to St George's Hospital, where she died the next day.

The house guest then turned up and, hearing the story, he – as readers will already have guessed – 'voted it all nonsense'. He insisted on sleeping in the room, and would ring on the servants' bell if anything untoward occurred at midnight. 'But,' he added, 'on no account come to me when I ring first; because I may be unnecessarily alarmed and seize the bell on the impulse of the moment. Wait until you hear a second ring.'

At midnight a single ring was heard from the room, which after a moment of silence became a cacophonous peal of bells. The householders hurried up to the room, where they found the guest lying in the same attitude as the maid. He survived his ordeal but would never speak of what he had seen.

Some correspondents pointed out that this account was suspiciously similar to a ghost story by Rhoda Broughton entitled 'The Truth, the Whole Truth and Nothing but the Truth', which was first published in 1868, and reappeared in a collection of 1872 called *Tales for Christmas Eve*. That story concerns '32 ---Street Mayfair'. The maid exclaims 'Oh my God, I have seen it!', an utterance that would recur in many of the purportedly true stories about the house. When it comes to the turn of the bold young man, he goes 'jumping up the stairs three steps at a time, and humming a tune'. But in this version it is he who is killed by the manifestation.

People continued to give their accounts of the house – or to make them up. Number 50 became a peg to hang a London ghost story on. There is the story of a room kept locked by the eccentric absentee landlord: every so often he would perplex the servants by turning up and locking them in the cellar while he spent a few hours in the room. And then there were the two sailors who broke into the house one night, and dossed down in one of the upper rooms. They saw a horrible shape moving stealthily about. One fled into the street just in time to see his companion leap screaming into the Square from the top storey.

Today, 50 Berkeley Square is the plush, tranquil home of Maggs Brothers, the antiquarian booksellers. I rang the bell and was admitted to the office. 'Did you know this house had a reputation for being haunted?' I asked one impeccably dressed young man. 'Yes, sir,' he said. He walked over to a cabinet from which he produced a photocopy of the relevant chapter from 'London Lore', saying, 'You can take this away with you if you like, sir.' I don't believe I've ever been given the brush-off in a politer way. Before leaving, I asked, 'I don't suppose anyone who works here has...you know...seen anything?' The man shook his head and smiled, and told me which button to press to open the front door and exit the building.

GHOST TRAINS

A good railway journey ought to lull the passenger into a dream state: the hypnotic motion, the flickering images beyond the window, the closed, unknowable faces of the other passengers. When my train from the North East approaches King's Cross, and glides through the soft gloom of those tunnels in which bells, like abandoned telephones, ring in relay for some mysterious operational purpose, I sometimes feel as though I am being roused from a long reverie.

The ghostliness of our railways has of course declined since the end of steam. British literary atmosphere in the classic era came from real fires, and steam locomotives were essentially real fires on the move, carrying with them their own mystery and metaphor in the form of the cloud of steam. The grimy diesel-hauled carriages of my own boyhood still had some possibilities. There were dimmer switches above the seats, for instance, so that passengers might set the atmosphere to their liking. But the modern network is over-rationalised. You can't get off a train without being warned that the 'platform surfaces' might be slippery; and all trains must be painted yellow at the front, so you can see them coming from a long way off. This is very unghostly, since the stealthiness of trains was part of their deadly glamour. In nineteenth century fiction trains were very often the instruments of death. In *Dombey and Son* (1846) by Charles Dickens, the villain, Carker, is run over by a train: a 'red-eyed monstrous express'. It 'licked up his stream of life with its fiery heat.' In *The Prime Minister* by Anthony Trollope (1876) the villain, Lopez, is 'knocked to bloody atoms' by a shrieking Scottish express going at 'a thousand miles an hour'.

The worst decade for railway accidents was the 1860's, when train numbers and speeds were outstripping safety provision. The worst of the decade occurred at Abergele in Wales, where runaway paraffin wagons – vehicles obviously emanating directly from some signalman's nightmare – collided with the Irish mail train from Euston. Thirty-three people were instantly immolated. Charles Dickens himself had always been wary of trains, and it is as though he brewed up a smash out of his own tremendous imagination. In 1865, he was riding on an express from

Folkestone to London that was derailed on a bridge at Staplehurst in Kent. Ten passengers were killed; Dickens's health and nerves were permanently undermined, and on subsequent train journeys he always clutched the armrests of the seat, feeling the carriage was 'down' on the right hand side. Shortly after the accident he wrote one of the earliest, and best, railway ghost stories, 'The Signalman'.

This sallow, neurotic functionary is practically in his tomb when the story begins, inhabiting as he does a signal box sunk in a dank cutting, where he is fixated on the adjacent tunnel mouth, and a glimmering red signal light. The narrator observes, 'So little sunlight ever found its way to this spot, that it had an earthy, deadly smell; and so much cold wind rushed through it, that it struck chill to me, as if I had left the natural world.' The signalman is tormented by a precognitive vision of a railway accident, and in an essay called 'Blood on the Tracks: Sensation Drama, Railways and the Dark Face of Modernity', Nicholas Daly sets the story in the context of Victorian railway accidents. Daly discovers in the popular perception of them something 'qualitatively different...they occur in "machine time", not human time. Human agency cannot usually move rapidly enough to intervene, and there are few rescues. In fact, such incidents are often too quick for the eye, and perception takes place after the event: if you see it, you are still alive.' It is this dimension that Dickens captures. The signalman sees the accident happen before it takes place. Here, as in the connection between spiritualism and radio, ghostliness is drawn from modernity rather than medieval demonology; or rather, the two are combined.

In the case of several nineteenth- or early twentieth-century railway accidents, the agency of a novelist is not in fact required. Straightforwardly factual accounts of the accidents read like ghost stories.

The Fall of the Tay Bridge

This occurred at the very ghostly time and on the very ghostly date of 7pm on Sunday December 28th, 1879. Naturally, a thunderstorm was raging. The Tay Bridge, which had been completed the year before, was the longest bridge in the world. It was latticed, like an infinitely prolonged and meandering seaside pier, and was frightening like a pier: both massive and whimsical, so that you wouldn't want to stand on the top and look down through the boards at the churning waters beneath. The doomed train was heading north to Dundee. At St Fort, at the south end of the bridge, all the seventy-five passengers' tickets were collected. This was a purely practical consideration: it was easier to collect the tickets while the passengers were still aboard the train than at Dundee, when they would all be disembarking. But it is hard to resist imagining some precognitive element here as well. The tickets, revealing place and approximate time of purchase would be used in the identification of the dead. (Some railway official would later make a collage of them all, and a reproduction of it appears on the first page of *Railway Ghosts*, edited by J.A. Brooks (1985). The tickets are arranged in a diamond shape, with photographs of four of the deceased placed in the four corners of the sheet of paper. It looks like the work of a disturbed seven year-old.)

As the train approached the bridge, the signalman at the southern end, Mr Barclay, had to give the driver of the engine a token – a pass giving him the right to traverse the single line. Such was the strength of the wind flying off the Firth that Mr Barclay had to approach the engine on all fours, and he retreated to his signal box in the same way. I imagine Mr Barclay, and his colleague Mr John Watt, standing in the box and looking into the brightly lit compartments as the train made its way onto the bridge. Picture the illuminated tableaux as they succeed one another: a single man reading in one compartment; a couple talking animatedly in another; a family disporting themselves variously in the third. I then imagine Mr Barclay and Mr Watt moving to a different window in the signal box, in order to watch the tail lights of the train as it progressed along the bridge.

They reported that a gust of wind shook the signal box; it was accompanied by a flash of dazzling light from the bridge...after which the tail lights of the train had gone. A sailor had been watching the train from a ship moored in the Firth. That same blast of wind had made him look away momentarily, and when he looked again there was no train and a gap in the bridge. Now if that blast of wind had been a literary device, it would have been a brilliant one. The same tasteful indirectness is evident elsewhere. A man called Maxwell, watching the lights of the train from his house on the north shore, saw three streams of fire fall from the bridge at the moment of the great gust, while villagers at Newport, north of the bridge, saw the water stop running from their taps, the main carrying the supply over the bridge having broken.

Seeing that their communication instruments had gone dead, Barclay and Watt struggled down to the shore of the Firth. 'As they stood there the moon momentarily broke through the flying cloud wrack and by its fitful light they saw to their horror that all the high girders had gone.' I quote L.T. C. Rolt, from his classic account of railway accidents, *Red For Danger* (1955). Rolt was a trained engineer, who also wrote some engaging memoirs, but I think he might have had the talent for a ghost story or two, as well.

Those railway officials at the south end of the bridge hoped the train had made it to the north, and vice versa. After the gap in the bridge became evident to the signalman at the north end of the bridge, he thought he saw a light on the south side of the gap – which he believed was the train retreating to St Fort and safety. It was never established what light he had really seen.

The locomotive – NBR 224 – lay at the bed of the Firth for three months, and sank twice more during the salvage operation. But it was discovered to be in good condition when brought to the surface, and it was returned to service. For years no driver would take it over the new Tay Bridge. Not until, on December 28th 1909, a crew – driver and fireman surely both arch-sceptics where the supernatural was concerned – worked the engine on the very same Sunday evening service as had ended in disaster exactly thirty-three years before. The men who drove number 224 had a nickname for her: 'The Diver.'

The accident formed the background of a folk tale written up as a ghost story by the Scottish writer Sorche Nic Leodhas. In 'The Man Who Missed The Tay Bridge Train' (1972) a young man lying ill in bed sends his 'fetch' – or his own living soul – to warn his lifelong friend not to board that particular train.

The Hawes Junction Crash

The railway accident that rivals the fall of the Tay Bridge for ghostliness occurred at Hawes Junction on the Settle-Carlisle stretch of the Midland Railway at the surpassingly ghostly time of 5am in the morning on Christmas Eve, 1910. Once again, the thunder storm had been laid on, and the gothic backdrop was in place. The Settle-Carlisle line runs through some of the wildest, most vertiginous landscape in Britain. When you travel along it, your ears pop as they do on an aeroplane. But the Johnny-come-lately Midland Railway was determined to have its own route to Scotland, and this was the only pathway left, the more sensible routes having been taken by its rivals. If this really were a ghost story, then the board of directors – urbane sophisticates in top hats – would have encountered a gnarled local during one of their fact-finding trips to the site of the proposed route. 'Begging your pardon sirs, but you can't be thinking of building a railway through these parts – the hills don't want it, and the hills will have their revenge!'

As it was, hundreds of navvies died during the construction of the fantastical viaducts and tunnels that the project required, and many crashes occurred after the line opened...

At Hawes Junction on that Christmas Eve, a harassed signalman let the St Pancras to Glasgow sleeper run into two engines he'd left standing on the line. He did not see the crash but a whistle was heard amid the storm, and a vague yet somehow decisive far-off rattle; a shepherd on a hillside saw a single flash of flame. The signalman turned to a colleague and said, 'Go to Bence [station master at Hawes Junction] and tell him I am afraid I have wrecked the Scotch Express', for which calmness of phrasing he earns my admiration.

The accident, in which nine people were incinerated, occurred just beyond the north end of Moorcock tunnel, near the highest point of the line. A couple of years ago, I spent a night alone in the station house at Dent, which is the stop just south of the accident site, and far remote from the village after which it is named. The house is now a holiday home, very comfortably furnished. But after the last train of the evening had gone, as the light faded and the wind rose, I became very conscious of the blackened railway sleepers that had been placed upright in the ground on the embankment above the station a hundred years ago to form a snow barrier. These lowered over the house, and they seemed subtly closer to it when I awoke suddenly at three o'clock in the morning than they had done at midnight when I'd turned in. I'm not sure that I would fancy renting Dent station on Christmas Eve, at least not alone.

*

The term 'ghost train' is – or was – used to describe a train which runs to test a schedule, or to keep a line clear of snow. Its most famous fictional use was in the title of Arnold Ridley's comedy-thriller play of 1923, inspired by a night he'd spent at Mangotsfield Station in Bristol, having missed the last train. The supposed train is a cover for gun running, and the station master's best line – delivered wide-eyed, and intended to frighten the occupants of the waiting room: 'Whatever it is, it never starts out at Truro, and it never runs into St Anne's. If it be a natural thing – where do it come from, and where do it go?' – killed for good the possibility of anyone writing a serious ghost train story.

Ridley went on to play Private Godfrey in *Dad's Army*. I once attended a *Dad's Army* special evening at the National Film Theatre, and this included a clip of Ridley being interviewed on tv about his play. He was very cynical about it, and much more ferocious than the mild-mannered and effete Private Godfrey. He said the play was just an attempt to supply the kind of rubbish that people appeared to want, a remark probably informed by the fact that his theatre company had gone bust in 1925, prompting him to sell the play for a pittance, only to see it become a staple of British theatre, and twice filmed.

A lyrical, and true ghost train account appears in a collection called *The Phantom Goods Train and Other Ghostly Tales from the Tracks* (1989), edited by W. Barry Herbert. It chronicles a series of sightings between 1917 and 1919 along a stretch of track from Dunphail to Dava in Morayshire. The percipients reported a very bright light, of unknown origin, and one man saw, riding beside the Plough constellation in the night sky, the image of a steaming locomotive pulling four cattle trucks. There is no particular pay-off to the story, but thirty years before, a train of forty cattle trucks had burned at Dava station, and all the cattle had been killed.

Ghost trains were popular in funfairs in the inter-war period, successors to the magic lantern phantasmagorias that featured in fairs from the late Eighteenth century. We think of ghost trains today as raucous thrill rides, but they were often satirical. The setting might be a moribund country halt, but rather than the station staff being merely slovenly and unhelpful they turn out to be cackling skeletons. A feature of the funfair ghost train might be the occupation of one seat by a suspiciously corpse-like passenger (a dummy of same I mean, of course), and the proximity to strangers that rail travel involves is one theme of railway ghost stories. This proximity was all the greater in the days when a passenger waiting on a dark and deserted platform could have resort to a waiting room.

Walter de la Mare's story, 'Crewe', which appears in his

collection *On The Edge* (1930), begins, irresistibly to my mind, 'When murky winter dusk begins to settle over the railway station at Crewe its first-class waiting room grows steadily more stagnant. Particularly if one is alone in it. The long-grimed windows do little more than sift the failing light that slopes in on them from the glass roof outside...And the grained massive black-leathered furniture becomes less and less inviting.'

But the narrator is not alone. He initially failed to notice a small man sitting in an 'obscure corner' of the waiting room and muffled up in a vast greatcoat. The man – a Mr Blake – begins by questioning the solidity of the waiting room, and of things in general. After warming his hands in the grate under the vast black marble fireplace, he embarks on a ghost story involving a sacked gardener, a suicide, and a scarecrow apparently advancing upon a country house. At the end of it, the narrator sees a train coming in along the adjacent platform, 'its gliding lighted windows patterning the platform planks. Alas, yet again it wasn't mine. Still, such is humanity, I preferred my own company just then.' And he steps out of the waiting room, preferring the 'dreadful gaseous luminosity of the platform' to the morbid reminiscences of Mr Blake.

If I ever wrote my own railway ghost story, incidentally, I would be tempted to borrow the title from a work of 1887 by Mary Louisa Molesworth: 'The Story of the Rippling Train'. This *is* a ghost story, and I began reading it with excitement, but the train in question turned out to be part of a lady's dress.

PART FOUR
'The lighting-up of the theatre'
& 'The infernal illusion'
or *The Crescendo* &
The Manifestation

THE CRESCENDO

Ghost stories, whether fictional or real, begin with a sof-
tening-up process in anticipation of the climactic revelation: a few preliminary, minor shocks, accumulating
strangeness.

In 'The Kit-Bag' (1908) by Algernon Blackwood, the
level-headed young barrister, Johnson, has begun for the
first time in his life to 'feel a little creepy'. Blackwood
writes, 'It is difficult to say exactly at what point fear
begins, when the causes of that fear are not plainly before
the eyes. Impressions gather on the surface of the mind,
film by film, as ice gathers upon the surface of still water,
but often so lightly that they claim no definite recognition
from the consciousness.'

Professor Richard Wiseman, psychologist at the
University of Hertfordshire, who believes there's 'some

interesting science' to be done about people's belief in ghosts, was recently quoted in the *Scotsman* as saying, 'You become afraid, you become hyper-vigilant, you detect something and then you become even more afraid. When we're afraid we suddenly become very good at monitoring our environment and our own physiology. That creaking door suddenly becomes important when normally you wouldn't notice it. And once that happens it becomes a positive feedback loop; you become even more scared, so then even more hyper-vigilant.'

This happened to me after Lizzie had told me the ghost story set down in Part One. I had rashly interviewed her (by phone) while spending the night alone in our dark rented house at the seaside. Lizzie had said she was sweating as she told me the story, and when I went to bed I too began to sweat. It just seemed so very likely that the little girl would speak to me, and the merest hint of a whispered, 'Hello Andrew' would have turned the universe on its head. I was sleeping under a duvet and a blanket. I threw the blanket onto the floor, and about three seconds later, I heard a bang from near the bed. Had I, in throwing the blanket into the darkness, disturbed some object on the floor which had then wavered for three seconds before falling over? That had *better* be it. I also kept seeing a flash of light towards the top of the curtain drawn over the window opposite the bed. Was the curtain moving in the slight breeze from the open window, and so intermittently letting in light from the street? My own room seemed to be conspiring against me, and I was reminded of the M.R. James story (and you really do not want to be reminded of his stories in the small hours) featuring a persecuted man whose own house becomes 'odious' to him.

I tried to take comfort from the deep breathing of the sea. But the sea is a ghostly zone, and no ally of the frightened human, and will one day be the death of us all. At 4.30 or so, I heard the birds begin to sing, and I tried to take comfort from that until the sun rose, the room filled with light, and I was able to sleep.

Logically, I suppose that I was haunting myself. In Dickens's ghost story, 'The Haunted House', the protagonist wakes at two in the morning to find he is sharing his bed with a skeleton. 'I sprang up and the skeleton sprang up also.' The man, it turns out, is speaking of his own skeleton, and the ghostly visions he pursues are all visions of his own early life. I had got into what Dickens in that story called 'a ghostly groove', which can happen just as easily with a number of people as with one individual. 'Everybody knows how contagious is fear of all sorts', writes Sheridan Le Fanu in 'An Account of Some Strange Disturbances in Aungier Street'. And group jeopardy is the dynamic of those ghost hunting TV programmes like *Most Haunted* in which at every lurching shadow or unexplained noise, people grab onto one another, and utter the only exclamation of shock permissible on mainstream TV: 'Omigod!'

In the state of hyper-vigilance, we become susceptible to the sort of flickering imagery of ghostliness. We have seen from Bram Stoker that 'the dead travel fast' and that spiritualism was akin to the speed of radio. The ghost story is a quick medium, stemming as it does from the medieval ballad, which employed a fast turnover of images. The best nineteenth-century ghost stories are full of subliminal images which gives them a modern, filmic quality. In 'To Be Taken With A Grain of Salt', the narrator is reading of a murder case:..

'I read it twice, if not three times. The discovery [of the body] had been made in a bedroom, and, when I laid down the paper I was aware of a flash – rush – flow – I do not know what to call it, – no word I can find is satisfactorily descriptive, – in which I seemed to see that bedroom passing through my room, like a picture impossibly painted on a running river. Though almost instantaneous in its passing, it was perfectly clear; so clear that I distinctly and with a sense of relief observed the absence of the dead body from the bed.'

This swiftness is evident in the title of a story of 1896 by Vincent O'Sullivan, 'When I Was Dead' (and the best thing about it *is* the title). Perhaps the most compressed opening to a ghost story is the following from 'The Man of Science' (1892) by Jerome K. Jerome...

'I met a man in the Strand one day that I knew very well, as I thought, although I had not seen him for years. We walked together to Charing Cross, and there we shook hands and parted. Next morning, I spoke of this meeting to a mutual friend, and then I learnt, for the first time, that the man had died six months before.'

(Unfortunately the narrator then changes the subject

and goes onto another, less interesting ghostly theme.)

It seems to me that we will not have time to guard against the instantaneous revelation. We can spend a life-time learning the laws of rationality, and they will be undone in less than a second. But we will try if at all pos-sible to shore them up, as I did alone in our rented house at the seaside; and in the early stages of ghost stories the central character will try to muster the forces of sanity and normality.

Scratching behind the skirting board will generally be put down to rats (a much less innocent explanation after the rodent-infested Great War than it had been before), whilst the flitting figure is an optical illusion or, as the Victorians more poetically had it, 'an ocular delusion'. A favourite of mine is from the accounts of phenomena at Borley Rectory. One of Price's academic observers felt a distinct tap on his shoulder while standing in the garden. He turned around, and there was nobody there. He surmised that it might have been 'a very heavy moth'. Here are half a dozen similar instances of wishful thinking or....

Six Attempts at Putting on a Brave Face

1. In *The Lost Stradivarius* (1895) by John Meade Falkner (which, along with *The Turn of the Screw* by Henry James, is one of the few successful ghost novels), John Maltravers, an Oxford student, senses a presence in his room every time he plays the Gagliarda (a fast and complicated dance) from a certain Italian violin suite of the mid-eighteenth century. In particular he seems to hear the sound of some-one sitting down in the wicker chair in his room when he begins the suite, and then rising from it when he has fin-ished. But, seeing nothing, he decides '...that there must be in the wicker chair osiers responsive to certain notes of the violin, as panes of glass in church windows are observed to vibrate in sympathy with certain tones of the organ.' (The Gagliarda, incidentally, symbolises the allure of a sort of aristocratic paganism, a dangerously seductive alternative to the crassness of evangelical Christianity).

2. In *A Christmas Carol* (1843), Scrooge declares to the ghost of his erstwhile business partner, Marley, that he does not believe in him even though he can see him. Marley asks, 'Why do you doubt your senses?' 'Because,' said Scrooge, 'a little thing affects them. A slight disorder of the stomach makes them cheats. You may be an undigested bit of beef, a blot of mustard, a crumb of cheese, a fragment of an underdone potato. There's more of gravy than of grave about you, whatever you are!'

3. In 'The Haunters and The Haunted' (1859) by Edward Bulwer-Lytton, the unnamed narrator has rented a known-to-be-haunted house situated a little way north of Oxford Street in hopes of seeing something 'perhaps excessively horrible'. He is in one of the drawing rooms with his man-servant when a chair spontaneously moves. 'Why, this is better than the turning tables', chuckles the new tenant, even as his dog begins howling in its distress. He surmises,

'...we have jugglers present, and though we may not discover their tricks, we shall catch them before they frighten us.'

4. In 'A View From a Hill' (1925) by M.R. James, Mr Fanshawe, who is of course 'a man of academic pursuits' is holding some old, peculiarly heavy binoculars he has come by while out walking in the country with his host, Squire Richards. Looking through these, at a certain hill called Gallows Hill, he clearly sees what he describes as 'a dummy gibbet and a man hanging on it.' Squire Richards responds that there's nothing on the hill but a wood and, looking again without the binoculars, Fanshawe sees that this is right: 'It must be something in the way this light falls.'

...Which is as near as I can come to finding the familiar, but in fact elusive, explanation, 'It must be a trick of the light.'

5. In 'A Visitor from Down Under' by L.P. Hartley, which was published in a collection called *The Ghost Book*, edited by Walter de La Mare in 1932, we are on the top deck of an open-topped bus 'making its last journey through the heart of London before turning in for the night'. The loquacious bus conductor encounters a silent, pale passenger with hat pulled down and collar up. 'Jolly evening,' says the conductor. (He is being ironic; it is wet and foggy). There is no reply from the passenger, who holds up his fare between the fingers of stiff, apparently immobile fingers. The conductor takes the money and goes back downstairs.

Later, the mysterious passenger is not there. The conductor never saw him come down the stairs, but he rationalises the situation with a very good example of sceptical wishful thinking: 'He must have got off with that cup-tie crowd'.

6. Early on in *The Green Man* by Kingsley Amis, which is another of the few successful ghost novels, Maurice Allington, the alcoholic landlord of the Green Man pub (he's on two bottles of whisky a day), sees a mysterious female figure in a part of the pub not open to the public. He turns aside for a moment to attend to other business, and when he looks back, she's gone. Later, the subject of this woman comes up in conversation: 'I realised for the first time that I had not subsequently seen that woman in the bar or the dining room or anywhere round the house. No doubt she had found the ladies' lavatory on the ground floor, and left while I was busy standing in for Fred...'

In real life, the rational explanation, on being earnestly sought is usually found. But perhaps it is a mistake to seek it. I myself would have a whole volume of ghost stories if I hadn't double checked.

Here are:

Two Ghosts that Rationality Dispelled
1. *The Late William*
William was a friend of mine who drank too much. I mean, most of my friends drink too much, but William seemed suicidal in the amount he put away. He lived, and

died, in a house that lay between my own house and my local high street. His front door opened directly on to the pavement, and I would often pass by just as he was stepping out of his house on his way to the pub. A year ago as I write, he came home from the pub, closed the door behind him, and collapsed in his hallway. The discovery of his body a few days later caused a big sensation in my area. It wasn't surprising that William had died, but he was such a garrulous, omnipresent figure in the local pubs and also (especially early in the evening) a very engaging talker, that his absence was keenly felt.

A month or so after his death, I was walking quickly past William's house when the front door opened, and he stepped onto the pavement. In the time it took me to see this, and to register the shock, I had moved a couple of paces beyond his door. I stopped, turned round, thinking: 'I know he's dead because I read his obituary last week', and stared at the man in the doorway. It wasn't William – not quite. It was a man who looked like him, and he was jangling the door keys in an official sort of way. He might have been an estate agent, or someone looking after William's estate or effects. So I had killed a good ghost story by turning back around. Another time, I did the same thing by waiting...

2. *The Boarded-Over Grave*
I was walking home from the pub, heading north along Swain's Lane, which divides the two equally ghostly parts of Highgate Cemetery. It was about 11.30pm. Looking

through the railings of the cemetery, I eyed the statue on a headstone of a small boy. As usual, he faced away, with a tension about his shoulders, just as though he might turn around at any moment. As is also usual with me, I stood still for a moment and dared the little blighter to turn around. He did not, thank God. I then noticed a grave was apparently being worked on in some way, and was covered with a six foot long piece of chipboard. As I looked on, the chipboard slowly lifted up. I held my ground, fighting off the heart attack that might be imminent, and...a fox crept out from the chipboard. That wasn't quite the end of the matter, since the fox sauntered up to the railings, and stared fixedly at me as if to say: 'You're a coward, aren't you?'

*

In Rudyard Kipling's 'My Own True Ghost Story' (1888) the narrator occupies a bungalow in India, and hears billiards being played in a room he knows to be empty. He is then informed by a servant that the place is indeed haunted. In the course of further enquiries, he discovers that this servant is prone to inventing ghost stories. Emboldened by this, the narrator listens hard when the billiards next start up, and pins the noise down to 'the wind and the rat and the sash and the window-bolt'. But he is half-regretful at the resolution: 'Had I only stopped at the proper time, I could have made ANYTHING out of it.'

POLTERGEISTS

There is what Brian Inglis called a 'strong family likeness' between poltergeists, and they have behaved in the same way over thousands of reported incidents across the world. They are also very *plausible* ghosts. They are a fine, counter-intuitive solution to the question of how a supernatural agency should behave. They make no attempt to embody the momentous implications of ghostliness. Instead, they specialise in irritating people. On the face of it, their repertoire is pathetically limited: they bang on floors and walls, pull hair, inflict minor blows, shift objects from place to place, speak (usually the same words over and over again), unmake beds, lift beds up, deposit debris on beds, and generally take a strong interest in beds. They are like the child who knocks on your door and then runs away, and part of your exasperation comes from trying to work out why they bothered. They are childish, or like petulant adolescents, and their presence in a house is often associated with the presence of adolescents or others experiencing emotional turmoil.

In fictional ghost stories, poltergeists usually play an ancillary role; they are the supporting act, creating the correct climate of fear for the main attraction: the manifestation. The poltergeists themselves generally do not manifest, being (as a rule) invisible. But they're often more frightening than the star turn.

Five Poltergeists

1. *Tedworth*

The template was set by the earliest well-known poltergeist

haunting, which is a sort of paradigm of childishness or petty spitefulness...

In the mid-1600s, a magistrate called Mr John Mompesson who lived at Tedworth in Wiltshire, which is now called Tidworth (even that name change is petty) confiscated and impounded a drum belonging to a man called William Drury. Drury was in effect a busker, who had been intimidating people into paying money for his performances on the drum. He was given over to the custody of a local constable, but soon released. However, he wanted his drum back, and John Mompesson wouldn't give it to him.

The story of what then occurred in Mr Mompesson's house was told a couple of decades later in 'Sadducismus Triumphatus' (1681), by Joseph Glanvill, who had visited the house and observed, or overheard, the haunting for himself. (The title is a refutation of the supposed beliefs of the New Testament-era Jewish sect, the Sadducees, who were said to have denied the immortality of the soul).

The house began to echo to the sound of knocking and drumming, especially in the small hours, and around the room where the confiscated drum was kept. The ingredient of emotional turmoil was perhaps supplied by Mrs Mompesson, who was in an advanced state of pregnancy when the disturbances began. (Others pointed the finger at a certain servant girl). Before the bursts of sound, the occupants would hear a 'hurling sound in the air over the house'. When Mrs Mompesson left the house to give birth, the noises ceased. But they resumed more intensely when she returned with the baby. Chairs 'walked' around rooms; the phrase 'a witch, a witch' was repeated more than a hundred times. Part of a bedstead was thrown, but fell as lightly as 'a lock of wool'. In his commentary on the haunting, Peter Underwood states of this article, 'It was noticed that it stopped exactly where it landed on the floor, not rolling or moving at all.' I have seen that kind of stopped motion when watching a scratched DVD, and it is quite disturbing enough then. The motion of objects thrown by poltergeists has consistently been reported as being slower and more controlled than the laws of physics would allow. (From Borley Rectory, Harry Price reported that objects must have flown around corners in order to move from their starting points to their end points.)

The Tedworth poltergeist 'purr'd in the children's bed like a cat' and poured the contents of chamber pots over these beds. The children would hear scratching under their beds, 'as if by something that had Iron Talons.' Seven or eight 'men-like' shapes were seen about the house. Mr Mompesson woke to see 'a great body with two red and glaring eyes'. (One of the the manifestations in 'An Account of Some Strange Disturbances in Aungier Street' by Sheridan Le Fanu has glaring red eyes).

It will already be evident that there was a kind of beauty in the story of the Tedworth haunting, but whether the credit belongs to the poltergeist itself or to the prose style of Joseph Glanvill I don't know. Certainly the word 'hurling' is just right for ghostliness, as is the idea of the chairs 'walking' around the room. The story is open-ended, which is also appealing. Drury admitted plaguing 'a man in Wiltshire', and would not call off the haunting 'till he hath made me satisfaction for taking away my drum.' He was tried for a witch. Glanvill writes, 'The fellow was condemned to Transportation, and accordingly sent away; but I know not how ('tis said by raising Storms and affrighting Seamen) he made shift to come back again.'

And on that uneasy note the story ends, but poltergeists have continued to behave in a similarly petty, obsessive-compulsive manner ever since, and there have been plenty of sequels to Tedworth.

2. *Little Burton*
There was for example the case of the poltergeist infestation at a house in Little Burton in Somerset in 1677: scratchings from under a bed, objects thrown onto beds, objects levitated. A disembodied hand and wrist manifested, as they later would in the séances of D.D. Home. In this instance, the hand held a hammer.

3. *Epworth*
In 1716 and 1717 there was poltergeist activity at Epworth Rectory in Lincolnshire, home to Samuel Wesley, father of John Wesley, among many other children. Samuel's wife and other family members wrote of latches lifted, sounds of rattling money, smashing glass, a gobbling turkey, deep groans; bursts of knocking going on interminably. And Mrs Wesley saw a manifestation: a badger-like thing, but

without a head – which is straight out of the M.R. James menagerie. The emotional energy here might have come from one of the daughters, Hetty, or marital differences between the Wesleys, arising from his Stuart sympathies and hers for William III. (They were a high-minded lot, of course, the Wesleys).

4. *Cock Lane*

The next in the sequence of famous poltergeists is the one at Cock Lane in East London. In 1759 a small house owned by a Richard Parsons, whose wife and daughter were both called Elizabeth, was let to a widower called William Kent and his sister-in-law, Fanny. When William was away for a night, Fanny, being nervous, asked young Elizabeth Parsons to share her bed. She was kept awake by what we now think of as the usual poltergeist racket, which became known in this case as 'Fanny scratchings'.

Meanwhile, William Kent had lent money to Richard Parsons, which Parsons was unable to repay. The two fell out. Kent moved to a different house, where Fanny died in 1760. Then the noises started up again in Cock Lane, and the Parsons family, and a servant girl of theirs, put it about that they had communicated with the poltergeist by means of codified rappings. From this they had learnt that the poltergeist was the spirit of Fanny, who wished it to be known from beyond the grave that she had been killed by William – a story to which William took great objection, not least because it was widely circulated.

The house in Cock Lane was the Borley Rectory of its

day, and it will already be apparent that it lacks the strangeness and mystery of the earlier poltergeist hauntings. It's too soap opera-ish; the human element is too pronounced. Kent indignantly asserted that his sister-in-law had died of smallpox, and the Parsons (and their servant) were prosecuted for defaming him.

5. *Worksop*

In 1896, a sceptical researcher called Frank Podmore (of whom more below) produced a report on poltergeists for the SPR. He interviewed witnesses in the case of a house in Worksop, home of a horse dealer called Joe White. There, kitchen utensils had begun flying around. Mr White sent for a doctor *and* the police. The doctor and Mrs White both saw a basin rise to the kitchen ceiling before falling to the floor. It is not known whether any policeman saw anything, and the phenomena stopped when Joe White's young lodger, Rose, left the house.

Podmore wrote of how the levitating objects had been described as moving through the air in a manner 'jerky, 'twirling', 'turning over and over'. When they landed they remained unbroken and 'rarely shivered'. He found the accounts of the witnesses convincing. Podmore was a sceptic, as I say, but earlier on, at another house-with-poltergeist, he himself had seen a picture frame slide along a mantelpiece. He commanded it to return 'in the name of the Trinity'. He saw it do so, but wrote this down as an illusion.

Overall, his position was that the co-incidence of

poltergeist effects with the presence in a house of troubled young people had to be telling; that the phenomena must be tricks played by those young people. My own response to that argument would be that those young people must have combined emotional turmoil with a perfect instinct for creepiness.

Or put it another way: poltergeists might be narrow specialists, but they are very good at what they do.

THE MANIFESTATION

In telling a ghost story it is quite easy to create the preliminary sense of unease, not least because the listener is usually very keen to be made uneasy. He will charitably assume that some terrific horror is coming, even though most climactic manifestations are a disappointment and do not justify the following sort of build-up, which is from *Hawksmoor* by Peter Ackroyd, a wonderfully creepy novel published in 1985, but set in the early eighteenth century:

> For those who wish the Sight of such ghosts and Apparitions I say this: it is of no long Duration, continuing for the most part only as you keep your Eyes steady (as I have done); the Timorous see merely by Glances, therefore, their Eyes always trembling at the sight of the Object, but the most Assured will fix their Look. There is this also: those who see the Daemon must draw down their eyes with their Fingers after.'

[153]

This is why shrewd ghost story writers often withhold the manifestation, instead making do with suggestive noises and the most fleeting glimpses of something or other. An example would be 'All Hallows' by Walter de la Mare, which, as already mentioned, concerns a remote cathedral taken over by diabolic forces. At the climax, these forces are confined within the cathedral, while the protagonists are on the roof: 'At that instant, a dull enormous rumble reverberated from within the building – as if a huge boulder or block of stone had been shifted or dislodged in the fabric; a peculiar grinding, nerve-wracking sound' – and one that challenges the reader to find the most horrible matching image. In 'At the End of the Passage' (1887) by Rudyard Kipling, the image of the ghost is captured, as if photographically, in its victim's eye, but the narrator does not tell us what form it takes. Mindful that the image alone was enough to kill the man, we do the rest of the work ourselves.

This kind of ending could be regarded as a cop-out, and it is usually the resort of a writer who is desperately fleeing from...

Six Ghosts of the Old School

1. *Headless Ghosts*

The narrator of 'The Haunters and The Haunted' by Edward Bulwer-Lytton dismisses a headless ghost as old hat when he says to his manservant, 'Remember in Germany how disappointed we were at not finding a ghost in that old castle that was said to be haunted by a headless apparition?...Well, I have heard of a house in London which, I have reason to hope, is decidedly haunted.' He means to sleep there that evening, hoping to see something 'perhaps excessively horrible'.

A headless man might not seem excessively horrible so much as unoriginal. In the excellent *Penguin Book of Ghosts* (2008) Jennifer Westwood and Jacqueline Simpson state that 'The headlessness of ghosts is a stereotype of popular ghost lore – at bottom, a shorthand way of talking about apparitions, like ghosts being dressed in white...' They reject the idea that most headless ghosts are those of people who have been decapitated by the executioner, and moreover they can prove it: 'Sir Thomas Boleyn of Bickling Hall, Norfolk, was not beheaded yet rides round in his phantom coach with his head beneath his arm.'

Headless-ness is associated with the riding of horses or the driving of phantom coaches. I once read, somewhere, the exhausted-sounding sentence, 'As usual, the horseman was headless.' Tarrant Ganville in Dorset is supposed to be haunted by William Doggett, steward in the eighteenth century of Eastbury House, the seat of Lord Melcombe. He committed suicide after being found out in a fraud, and is said to appear headless while riding on a coach pulled by headless horses and driven by a headless coachman. The question arises: *How could they see where they were going?* The *reductio ad absurdum* is reached at Whitby in Yorkshire, where a team of headless horses driven by a headless coachman are said to ride along the cliff adjacent to the ruined Abbey before toppling over the edge.

2. *Phantom Coaches*

In folklore these might symbolise the territorial arrogance of a lord of the manor when driven fast and recklessly. Sir Laurence Tanfield, a rapacious landlord at Burford and the surrounding area in Oxfordshire, was known as 'The Wicked Lord'. The legend that grew up after his death in 1625 was that he and his wife drove in a flying coach over the roofs of the houses in Burford, which the locals found 'a nuisance', not least because a sighting of the coach meant death. Seven priests came to lay the ghost or ghosts. Katherine Briggs, the folklorist, reported in the 1960's that this had been done by 'reading them small', using injunctions from scripture. The ghost of Lady Tanfield was thus confined to a bottle, which was thrown in the river. The coach itself was safely garaged under a certain arch of the river bridge, but it might escape if ever the river ran dry under that arch. Once the river did run dangerously low, and the water began to seethe and bubble.

In spite of all these precautions, Sir Laurence and his coach continued to drive along a particular road in Whittington in Gloucestershire, and when, late in the nineteenth century, a man was found dead on that road, it was said that he must have caught sight of The Wicked Lord.

In the above-mentioned *Phantasms of the Living*, the painfully rigorous authors find it hard to classify sightings of phantom coaches, of which there have been many, often by more than one person at a time. As we have seen, the authors of that book believed that apparitions were the result of one person communicating a sense of his or her-self telepathically to another at a moment of crisis. The authors found awkward the fact that sometimes the com-municants chose to convey the image of a coach as well as, or instead of, their own likeness. The presentation of this additional element is problematic, just as the sending of a large attachment with an email frequently is. How can the sending of an image of a coach be justified? What is so special about the coach? The authors reach no firm con-clusion, but some accounts of coach sightings are provid-ed, and they have the creepiness that is the keynote of that wonderful book. In one case, a vehicle passed a window absolutely silently on gravel; the coachman and the foot-man on the exterior of the carriage had black faces. In India, a Mr Paul Bird, resident of 39, Strand, Calcutta, 'followed a phantom gharri for 100 yards, into the very portico of Hastings House at Alipore, while the same vehi-cle was watched in its approach by his wife from a win-dow.'

3. *White Ladies* etc

White Ladies are beautiful aristocratic women dressed in white. They are wistful, hand-wringing types who perpetu-ate the memory of some sleight or loss suffered in their lives. They are associated with water, and there is a White Lass Beck near Thirsk in Yorkshire. The legend grew up at Longnor in Shropshire of a white lady rising from a deep pond known as the Black Pool. We have already men-tioned the white lady at Pluckley in Kent, and there are at least a dozen others firmly entrenched in British folklore. There are a couple of grey ladies too. Grey ladies are white ladies that have run in the wash. Well, I'm afraid that these pious phantoms do attract flippancy. There is a Green Lady at Thorpe Hall, near Louth in Lincolnshire, and then there is the Brown Lady at Raynham Hall, Norfolk, which is one of the most famous British ghosts in that it was photographed.

It was first seen during Christmas 1835, by a Colonel Loftus, a family guest of the Townshend family, owners of the Hall. He described her as being of noble bearing, and brown. (She was wearing a brown satin dress, that is). Oh, and she didn't have any eyes. Other house guests said that they too had seen the figure in the same room. Colonel Loftus sketched the apparition, and an artist made a painting from the sketch, which was hung in the house. It was speculated that the ghost must be that of Dorothy Walpole, the sister of Britain's first Prime Minister, Sir Robert Walpole. In about 1713 she married Charles Townshend, and he treated her badly. She may also have been the mistress of the rakehell Lord Wharton.

A few years after the first sighting, Captain Marryat, naval commander and author of children's historical adventures, including *The Children of the New Forest*, visited Raynham Hall. Like the bold young man in 'The Truth, The Whole Truth and Nothing But The Truth' and a dozen other hero/idiots of ghost stories, Captain Marryat immediately plumped for the haunted room when given his choice of sleeping quarters. (Well, he *had* won the

Royal Humane Society's gold medal for bravery during his naval career). He and two companions were walking along the corridor from which that room lead when the Brown Lady appeared. All three saw her, and Captain Marryat did what any red-blooded Englishman would do on seeing a ghost: he took out his revolver and shot it. The bullet flew into a door and the figure disappeared.

On September 19th, 1936, two photographers from *Country Life* magazine – a Captain Provand and Mr Indre Shira – were photographing the main staircase at Raynham Hall when the Brown Lady appeared on the stairs. The resulting photograph shows a transparent, vaguely human shape, more white than brown. The Brown Lady has not been seen since, fading away along with all the Captains and Colonels who could announce that they had seen her in the confident expectation of being believed.

4. *Black Dogs*

Black dogs are bad news. Winston Churchill called his depression his Black Dog. As ghosts, they are particularly East Anglian, and a sighting of them portends death. I was walking out of a gift shop in Walberswick in Suffolk having just bought a copy of Martin Newell's story-poem, *Black Suck, The Ghost Dog of Eastern England* (1999), when a big black Labrador walked directly up to me. But I thought I might have earned a let off since it was carrying a yellow tennis ball in its mouth. Actually, the black dog of folklore is a shaggy beast with flaming red eyes, and generally not a Labrador. I mean, if you threw a stick for it, you'd be dead by the time you shouted 'Fetch!'

In his introduction to his poem, Newell writes, 'The dog has many names. He's known in some places as Galleytrot and in others as The Barguest or Old Snarleyow. Certain villages know him as Scarp, Trash or Rugusan. Most commonly he's called Old Shuck or Black Shuck.' He haunts 'bridges, fords and the boundary lines of ancient parishes.' He is 'as big as a calf'. The black dog came over with the Norsemen, being the black hound of their God Odin. Newell is interesting on the etymology of 'Shuck'. It possibly derives from the Old English word 'sceocca' meaning 'terror' or 'Satan', and of course it's similar to shock. It should perhaps be reintroduced to denote a fright that is like a shock, only worse – the kind of shock you can die of.

5. *Radiant Boys*

Radiant boys are a minor ghost genre, and I include them here partly because I like the name. Two principal ones have been recorded. The first was seen by 'The Reverend Henry A ----' when he was staying at Corby Castle in Cumberland in September 1803. He awoke in the middle of the night to see by his bed 'a glimmer that suddenly increased to a bright flame'. He then perceived 'a beautiful boy, clothed in white, with bright locks resembling gold'. The boy remained 'some minutes'; his expression was benevolent. He then glided towards the side of the chimney and disappeared. The next morning, desperate to quit the house, the percipient summoned his carriage with such urgency that its driver knocked down part of a wall on his approach to the front door. But Henry A--- later gave an account in writing of what he'd seen, and it appears in 'The Night Side of Nature' (1848), by Mrs Catherine Crowe.

The other reason I am interested in radiant boys is that one was seen by Viscount Castlereagh. I studied Castlereagh for history 'A' level. His political career ran in parallel with that of George Canning. They were both brilliant lieutenants of Pitt the Younger, and both made their name as foreign secretaries, although Canning was also briefly prime minister. Castlereagh and Canning were opposed like two people in a novel, and in 1809 they fought a duel over the correct conduct of the Napoleonic War. As foreign secretary, Castlereagh was neurotic and cautious. He wanted to create a European-wide alliance against Napoleon. Canning was more cavalier, and believed that Britain's best interests would be served by remaining aloof.

At school we were told that Canning was the dashing, interesting one. But whereas Canning had merely inhabited the above-mentioned 50 Berkeley Square before it gained its haunted reputation, Castlereagh had actually seen a ghost.

He told the story to Sir Walter Scott in Paris in 1815, describing the vision 'with great minuteness'. According to Scott, 'It was a naked child, which he saw slip out of the grate of a bedroom while he looked at the decaying fire. It increased at every step it advanced towards him, and again

[161]

diminished in size till it went into the fireplace and disappeared. I could not tell what to make of so wild a story told by a man whose habits were equally remote from quizzing or inventing a tale of wonder.'

On August 12 1822, Castlereagh killed himself by slitting his carotid artery with a penknife. He was Leader of the House of Commons as well as Foreign Secretary at the time and, according to the Duke of Wellington, he had been 'in a state bordering insanity' as a result of the stress of defending in the House the repressive policies of the Prime Minister, Lord Liverpool, at a time of economic depression and working class unrest.

(George Canning, feeling 'quite knocked up' at the effort of trying to put together a ruling coalition, died in 1827.)

6. *Monks and Nuns*

It's not hard to see how monks and nuns become ghostly. They have spiritual gravitas, and they look the part, with their cowls and loose robes. They are prone to being walled up alive (a practice always more likely to occur in fiction than in fact) and are unworldly to begin with — halfway to being ghosts in life, you might say. Any sexual liaison they have will necessarily be illicit and probably fraught, and on both counts the attendant emotions might endure. (In that she had engaged in a love affair, the Borley Rectory nun was an absolutely orthodox ghost.)

Any private house that had been seized from a religious order during the Reformation is ripe for a haunting. The above-mentioned Markyate Cell is a case in point. Abbey House at Cambridge is another. It was built on the site of an Augustinian Priory, and a female figure in nun's clothes was seen there in the first half of the twentieth century.

My father, visiting Rievaulx Abbey in Yorkshire in the late nineteen-eighties, fell into conversation with the Abbey caretaker who told my dad as a matter of absolute certainty that a cowled figure hovered above the highest surviving arch of the monastery on certain nights. My father provided all the usual character references on behalf of this man: 'Lovely chap; intelligent, charming and straight as a die.'

PHANTASMS OF THE LIVING

We come now to a more evolved sort of ghost than the essentially medieval ones mentioned above.

The psychical researchers of the late nineteenth century shifted their interest from objective to subjective ghosts, just as the ghost story writers would do a few years later. As already stated, *Phantasms of the Living* is the title of a two-volume book published in 1886 and written by Edmund Gurney, Frederic Myers and Frank Podmore, all members of the Society for Psychical Research. It is a study of what were called 'crisis apparitions': phantasmal appearances before the living of people on the brink of death.

'After considering over two thousand accounts of experiences that our informants regarded as inexplicable by ordinary laws,' state the authors in their introduction, 'we find that more than half of them are narratives of appearances or other impressions coincident either with the death of the person [seen in ghostly form] or with some critical moment in his life history.' They add that the value of accounts of apparitions of people who died some time before – ghosts as conventionally understood – are lessened by the fact there is usually no corresponding and verifiable event that can be connected to them. The accounts can be dismissed as 'merely morbid or casual – the random and meaningless fictions of an over-stimulated eye or brain.'

But 'if we can prove that a great number of apparitions coincide with the death of the person seen, we may fairly say, as we do say, that chance alone cannot explain this coincidence, and that there is a causal connection between the two events.'

The cause of the visions is considered by the authors to be thought transference or telepathy – 'the supersensory action of one mind on another'. To transmit one's thoughts one is required to be alive, even if only just. In fact, the higher state of consciousness presumed to be associated with a 'crisis' state is considered more likely to trigger such projection.

This is the working assumption of most of the book, and it suited the SPR's keenness to distance itself from the mediums whose work was concentrated in the posthumous sphere. But in spite of the upbeat word 'living' in the title, the book is permeated with the beautiful melancholy of a winter Sunday when the rain has set in, and two of its three authors would commit suicide. (Edmund Gurney, musician and psychologist, died of an overdose of narcotic medicine in 1888. Frank Podmore, founding member of the Fabian Society, and civil servant at the Post Office, was found dead in a pond on a golf course near Malvern in 1910).

The book is the first great statement of the SPR. It is limpidly written, and exhaustively subdivided. Visions seen by multiple 'percipients' are included, as are those seen in dreams or on the 'borderland' of dreams. There are auditory and tactile cases as well as purely visual ones. The seven hundred or so cases are differentiated from the authors' commentary by appearing in smaller print, like the cases in a legal text book, and almost all have the strangeness that is a hallmark of the plausible. I doubt that there is a more ghostly book in the entire British Library.

I quote one auditory case in full – a 'remarkably clear instance of the direct reproduction of the agent's sensation in the percipient's consciousness', recorded by Joan R. Severn of Brantwood, Coniston:

Years ago, in Scotland, at my own home, I was in the drawing room with my mother and aunt; the latter was busy writing at a table in the middle of the room, facing my mother, who was on a sofa sewing, while I was quietly amusing myself in my own way. It was all very quiet, when suddenly I was much startled by my mother, who gave a scream and threw herself back on the sofa, putting both her hands up to cover her ears, saying, 'Oh, there's water rushing fast into my ears, and I'm sure either my brother, or son James, must be drowning, or both of them!' My aunt Margaret jumped up, and was rather angry and said, 'Catherine, I never heard such nonsense, how can you be so foolish!' My aunt seemed vexed and ashamed it should happen before me, for I was very frightened, and remember it all so vividly. My poor mother cried, saying, 'Oh, I know it's true, or why would this water keep rushing into my ears?'

Alas! It proved too true, for very soon I could see people running very hard towards the bathing-place, and I remember the shudder that then ran through me, and the hope that my mother would not look out of the windows. Soon my uncle came hurrying to the house very white and distressed; all he could say was, 'hot blankets!', but it was too late – poor James was drowned. He was 21 years old, and my mother's eldest child. Both the other witnesses of this scene are dead.'

[A footnote reads: 'The narrator's brother, James Agnew, was drowned while bathing in the River Bladnoch. The date, as we find from a copy of an inscription in Wigtown churchyard, was June 8, 1853.']

I choose this partly because it sounds true, and partly because it is so very like the beginning of the brilliant film, *Don't Look Now* (1973), directed by Nicolas Roeg from a Daphne du Maurier short story, in which a drowning is

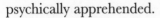

psychically apprehended.

This exhaustive chronicling of death wraiths or crisis apparitions did not make these apparitions too self-conscious to continue appearing, and the most famous one did so on June 22nd 1893. On that day, Admiral Sir George Tryon was aboard HMS *Victoria*, the flagship of the British Mediterranean Fleet, of which he was the commander. Sailing between Beirut and Tripoli, he signalled for the two columns of ships he was leading to turn towards each other so as to approach Tripoli in tighter formation. But he had miscalculated the gap, and a ship called HMS *Camperdown* rammed HMS *Victoria*, which quickly sank, killing Tryon and many of his men. As the ship went down, he is reported to have said, 'It is entirely my fault' – a remark that would have been of no help to anyone.

At that precise time, Admiral Tryon is said to have appeared at an 'At Home' given by his wife, Lady Tryon, at Eaton Square. He walked across the drawing room speaking to nobody. His wife, being distracted with the business of a hostess, did not see him but several guests did.

Admiral Tryon was right about the accident being his fault, and the question of why he gave the order he did takes up as much space in the accounts of the case as the details of the manifestation. The sceptic, incidentally, would point out that his appearance at the party coincides too neatly with the myth that a sailor's 'fetch' or spirit would alert his family to his death.

It must also be admitted that people would be more

likely to make up – or to believe – a crisis apparition story in those days than they would be today. Some of the cases in *Phantasms of the Living* arise from what is described in one as the 'time-worn arrangement' between friends: that 'whichever died first would endeavour to visit the other'. That sort of arrangement isn't so popular in 2009. Hardly anybody today has heard of a crisis apparition, but I believe the notion was still widespread in the early Seventies, when the French film, *The Wages of Fear* (1953) was shown on British TV...

It's about two men employed to drive lorries carrying explosives to the scene of an oil well fire in a remote South American town. The explosives will be used to put out the fire – but there's every chance that they'll blow up the lorries on the way. One of the pair, having successfully accomplished his mission, celebrates by swerving about on a mountain road. This causes him to crash fatally, at which exact moment his girlfriend suddenly sits bolt upright in bed.

The day after the film was broadcast, I was kicking a tennis ball about in the suburban cul-de-sac in which I grew up, and discussing it with the kid who lived over the road, whose name was Allan. He was a year or two older than me – thirteen or thereabouts – so I expected him to be more worldly and authoritative on most subjects. Even so, I was surprised by the crispness of his diagnosis of that scene. 'She had a telepathic hallucination. That often happens when someone you know dies.' His own father, Ray, died shortly afterwards while at work, and my first thought

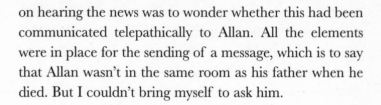

on hearing the news was to wonder whether this had been communicated telepathically to Allan. All the elements were in place for the sending of a message, which is to say that Allan wasn't in the same room as his father when he died. But I couldn't bring myself to ask him.

A Q&A OF PHANTOMS

What is the purpose of ghosts?

It is easier to classify ghosts by the form they take (see above) than by their purpose. For example, while most white ladies are benign, some are death omens, and while most black dogs are death omens, some − like the admittedly unusually small and well-behaved black dog seen in company with the Grey Lady associated with Levens Hall in Westmorland − are harmless. You might as well ask, 'What is the purpose of human beings?' And some ghosts, like some humans, have no purpose. Take those raised or pursued by the spiritualists of the nineteenth century. The point of these spirits was solely to confirm that spirits existed. If they communicated a message it was, as we have seen, so that they could prove they had once been alive, or to offer their best wishes to everyone and to tell them not to worry, since being dead wasn't half as bad as they might think. This is also true of those ghosts that appear as a result of a pact between two people: 'Whoever dies first will appear to the other.' As we have seen there was a fashion for these in the late nineteenth century, but there are earlier examples. Madame Beauclair, mistress of

[169]

James II, and the Duchess of Mazarine, who had been the mistress of Charles II, had such an arrangement. The Duchess was the first to die, and she did appear to Madame Beauclair at St James's Palace, albeit rather tardily after the interval of a few years.

The myriad of medieval ghosts generally did have a purpose, as already noted. Since everyone expected them to appear, appearance itself was not enough. There had to be a point. In the previously mentioned story, 'Crewe', by Walter de la Mare, the irritating sage, Mr Blake says, 'And what about that further shore? It's my belief there's some kind of ferry plying on that river. And coming back depends on what you want to come back for.'

Taking a run at it, you might say that ghosts with a purpose from whatever period are concerned either with themselves primarily or with the percipient. The first kind, the egotistical ghosts, might walk the earth in memory of a wrong they've suffered or a wrong they did, or because they were buried in the wrong place. Even after the church had largely dismissed the possibility of ghosts, it conceded that spirits awaiting their destination might linger on earth. The effect of seeing this kind of introspective ghost might be profound, but that would be co-incidental. The landlord of the Gatehouse pub in Highgate, which is about a quarter of a mile from my home, and partly late-medieval, suffered a heart attack in 1947 after seeing a man-like shape moving about in the cellar. The figure communicated nothing to him except the heart attack.

The purposeful ghosts, those ghosts concerned with the

percipient, might function as a death omen, give a warning, advise, encourage or instruct. In their case, the ghost story does not end with their appearance. It ends with the effect of their appearance: the conversion of Scrooge, for example. Or they might, like Hamlet's father, seek revenge for their murder. Most stories of this latter kind are bloodthirstily orthodox, but there's a more elliptical one in *Haunted England* by Christina Hole. She quotes from the *Gentleman's Magazine* of 1774, which recounted the story of a fourteen year old schoolboy called John Daniel. He attended Beaminster School, which was held in part of the parish church. He was a sickly boy, and suffered from fits.

One day in May 1728, he went out for a walk and did not return. His body was found in a field, and it was assumed he'd had a fit. He was mourned over, and duly buried. About a month later, after school had finished for the day, some of the schoolboys heard the sound of a man walking about the church with heavy boots, but they could see no man. They ran out into the churchyard, from where they heard the minister preaching and psalms being sung in the church, which they knew to be empty. They then walked past an open door that gave onto their classroom (I like this flowing, filmic succession of scenes by the way) in which they saw a coffin and John Daniel sitting up in it. Several boys saw him. One of them was new to the school; he had not known John Daniel in life, but he later give an accurate description of him.

The boys reported that John Daniel had a bandaged hand, which indeed he had done at the time of his death, although this had not been widely known. One of the observers was the dead boy's half brother. He said, 'There sits our John', and threw a stone at him calling, 'Take it!' whereupon the image disappeared.

On the strength of this, the body was disinterred and an inquest held upon it. A black mark was found about John Daniel's neck and a verdict of 'Strangled' was brought in, although no-one was ever convicted of the crime.

Ghosts often try to interfere in the criminal justice, or at any rate the psychics who purport to communicate their messages do. Not long after the Portuguese police began their investigation into the disappearance of Madeleine McCann they had accumulated two dossiers 8cm thick filled with communications from psychics.

Can Ghosts Eat?

'Wandering Willie's Tale' is a ghost story inset into Sir Walter Scott's novel, *Redgauntlet* (1824). It tells of Steenie Steenson, a poor tenant farmer who, while still alive, visits his former landlord, the recently-deceased Sir Robert Redgauntlet, in hell, to ask for a receipt for the rent he paid him. Sir Robert, sitting before a great banquet, says, 'Ye maun eat and drink – for we do little else here'.

There are two things to say about that. Firstly, Sir Robert makes hell sound remarkably like modern Britain and secondly, he may be trying to trap Willie, mindful of the rule of the Fates in Ancient Greece, which said that anyone who ate or drank in the underworld would be con-

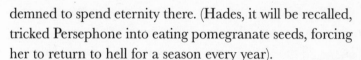

demned to spend eternity there. (Hades, it will be recalled, tricked Persephone into eating pomegranate seeds, forcing her to return to hell for a season every year).

In *Macbeth*, Banquo's ghost comes to the feast but does not eat. In *A Christmas Carol*, the ghost of Christmas past beckons Scrooge while seated before a banquet of 'turkeys, geese, game, poultry, brawn, great joints of meat, sucking-pigs, long wreaths of sausages, mince-pies, plum puddings, barrels of oysters, red hot chestnuts, cherry-cheeked apples, juicy oranges, luscious pears, immense twelfth-cakes...' – none of which he touches. Nor does he drink the punch that 'made the chamber dim with its delicious steam.'

In 'Uncle Cornelius His Story' (1869) by George MacDonald, Uncle Cornelius, a 'very tall, very thin, very pale' man who 'was a student of all those regions of speculation in which anything to be called knowledge is impossible', mentions that 'the disembodied are said to be able to drink, if not eat. I must confess, however, that, although well attested, the story is to me scarcely credible. Fancy a glass of Bavarian beer lifted into the air without a visible hand, turned upside down and set empty on the table!'

However, when L.P. Hartley referred to the question of whether a ghost could eat or drink in his introduction to *The Third Ghost Book*, edited by Lady Cynthia Asquith (1955), he wrote, 'I can't quote an instance, but I shouldn't be surprised to come across a modern ghost who could do both.'

I thought I had found one in Algernon Blackwood's story, 'Keeping His Promise' (1906). This concerns a young man called Field, a friend of another young man called Marriott, who arrives unannounced at Field's rooms in Edinburgh. He is in need of food and drink, and Field serves him a brown loaf, scones and marmalade, and cocoa. Field eats 'like an animal', and later turns out to have been dead at the time of doing so. But it also turns out that the food remained all along in Field's larder, and that the whole meal had been illusory.

I once wrote a ghost story called 'The Wayfarer', which was read on Radio Four in a series marking the centenary of the founding of the Caravan Club. The ghost − that of an Edwardian pioneer of caravanning − eats lemon cake and drinks tea, but this was a mistake on my part.

What Do Ghosts Wear?

I might have made a faux pas here as well. My friend David, the ghost story connoisseur, and I once made a short film of a ghost story we'd concocted. Out ghost would wear working class street clothes, including a track suit top. I was in charge of the props, and on the second day of shooting, I forgot to bring the ghost's clothes. I said to David, 'Not to worry, I'll just go to Oxfam and buy a similar sort of top to the one we used yesterday', at which he said (very mildly in the circumstances), 'So this will be the first ever ghost with a change of clothes?'

But I think that ghosts *might* change clothes...

Those SPR stalwarts who argued that ghosts were telepathic transmissions dealt breezily with the question of clothes. The agent who transfers the apparition (the sender of the telepathic message) does so in order that it should be recognised by the percipient. The 'normal appearance' of the figure is projected. If any such apparition makes more than one appearance, the clothes don't necessarily have to be the same on both occasions, as long as they are within the range of the 'normal appearance' of the figure as known to the percipient.

Of course the traditional ghost wore, or indeed *was*, a white sheet. In contemporary productions of *Macbeth*, Banquo's ghost wore a white sheet. In *Hamlet*, Horatio recalls the prelude to the assassination of Julius Caesar: 'The graves stood tenantless and the sheeted dead/Did squeak and gibber in the Roman streets'. The sheet is taken to be a shroud. In 'Oh, Whistle and I'll Come to You' by M.R. James, the ghost is a possessed bed sheet, and has a horrible 'face of crumpled linen'. (In Jonathan Miller's film of the story, the effect is beautifully captured and accompanied by a sort of blaring sea monster noise).

In the above-mentioned book by Sir Oliver Lodge, *Raymond: Or Life and Death*, Lodge recorded that, during one séance conversation with his dead son, the boy was asked what sort of clothes people wore on the other side. The medium's unsophisticated and child-like female spirit control – through whom Raymond was speaking – stumbled over the answer: 'They are all man-u-factured' she/ he said. The message from Raymond went on: 'Can you fancy me in white robes? ...[A fellow] may make up his mind to wear his own clothes a little while, but he will soon be dressing like the natives.'

Are Ghosts Seen By More than One Person at a Time?

Yes. In the jargon of *Phantasms of the Living* these sightings are categorised under 'multiple percipients'. From my reading of collections of true ghost stories, I would say that about thirty per cent of apparitions are seen by more than one person, and these are usually given pride of place at the start of the book. If, in sophisticated fictional ghost stories, the ghost is seen by only one person, that's an indication that the sighting is subjective; that the ghost is psychological. In *The Turn of the Screw* (1898) by Henry James, the troubled governess at a lonely country house is haunted by visions of her predecessor, Miss Jessel. When she sees Miss Jessel standing on the opposite side of a lake, she tries to make her fellow-servant, Mrs Grose, see her too: 'She's as big as a blazing fire! Only look, dearest woman, look - !' But she does not succeed.

In true ghost stories, the numbers of percipients range upwards until we reach the point of mass-hallucination, at which we come back to the question of psychology. The best known instance is the Angel of Mons. The retreat from Mons in Belgium in August 1914 was the first indication that Britain would not win the war quickly. The full horror of what had started was beginning to become apparent, and this was a scenario traumatic enough to produce a ghost or ghosts. An Angel, protecting the British

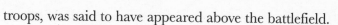

troops, was said to have appeared above the battlefield.

It is thought that this vision was created retrospectively, so to speak, following the publication of a story by Arthur Machen in the *Evening News* on September 29th 1914. This depicted the ghosts of the bowmen of Agincourt arriving on the Western Front to fire arrows at the German lines that killed without leaving wounds. In his book, *The Great War and Modern Memory*, Paul Fussell writes that Machen described these bowmen, who appeared between the two armies, as:

> a long line of shapes, with a 'shining' about them. It was the shining that did it: within a week Machen's fictional bowmen had been transformed into real angels, and what he had written as palpable fiction was credited as fact. Machen was embarrassed and distressed by the misapprehension, but he was assured, especially by the clergy, that he was wrong...

It is interesting that Machen should have been embarrassed at the way his story was taken literally. He was a Welsh mystic with Druidic tendencies, very much the theatrical occultist; he had long white hair and wore cloaks. His story, 'The Great God Pan' (1890), about a brain operation gone wrong, is a classic of horror that had a lasting effect on Stephen King. 'The Bowmen' is echoed in another of his stories, 'Munitions of War' (1915), in which a reporter travels by train through fog towards the beautiful old town of Westpool to see how it is facing 'the stress of war'. He finds that the place has 'a shy, barred-up air'.

It is apparently demoralised, doing nothing for the war effort. He wakes in the middle of the night, and looks out of his hotel window towards the Middle Quay, where he sees a vast enterprise going on, involving the loading of 'great ships, faint and huge in the frosty mists' by men speaking to one another in old-fashioned slang. He over-hears one of them announce, while bantering with a fellow worker, 'I fell at Trafalgar!'

Can There Be Ghosts of Inanimate Objects?

Yes. We just have to think of Macbeth and 'Is this a dagger which I see before me...' And we have seen the problem that phantom coaches caused to the believers in ghosts as telepathic messages. They have also got ghost trains to reckon with and at least one bus, according to a report in the 'Morning Post' of June 16th 1934...

At an inquest, held in Paddington on June 15th 1934, into the death in a motor accident of Ian James Beaton of Dollis Hill, witnesses described the scene of the accident – the junction of St Mark's Road and Cambridge Gardens – as dangerous because of a ghost double-decker. It had been heard at night, roaring towards the junction 'long after the regular bus service had stopped'. The bus was described as brightly illuminated, which goes for many of the inanimate objects that have manifested. They tend to be smaller than buses, and of the order of radiant chandeliers, candles, fireworks, balls or jewels.

But the best inanimate ghost that I have read of is that of a house, and for this we must re-visit *Apparitions and*

Haunted Houses by Sir Ernest Bennett. The account was sent to him by Miss Ruth Wynne of Rougham Rectory, Bury St Edmunds. One 'dull, damp' afternoon in October 1926, she was walking through fields with 'her pupil', aged fourteen, on the way to have a look at the church in the neighbouring village of Bradfield St George. They did not know the area and, emerging from the fields, they came to some high trees. They both saw beyond the trees a part of the roof of a stucco house and Miss Wynne recalls seeing 'some windows of Georgian design'. They went on to the church and came back by a different way.

The two did not take the same route until next spring. Again it was a dull afternoon, but with good visibility. As they emerged from the fields, the pair simultaneously cried, 'Where's the wall?' The trees were there, but beyond lay nothing but 'a wilderness of tumbled earth'. They thought the house and wall must have been pulled down, but closer inspection showed ponds on the site that had obviously been there a long time. Enquiries among the villagers revealed no knowledge of a house ever having stood on the spot. Miss Ruth Wynne concludes her account by asserting that she is now 'what you might call psychic and this is the only experience of the kind I have ever had'. Her pupil, she added, was 'neither imaginative not suggestible', and was sufficiently good friends with her to disagree firmly with her if she wished to do so.

I find this story moving and strange: the two females walking abroad, seeking out experiences of life that the mistress might explain to the pupil...and yet they are reduced to equality by this impenetrable enigma.

FIVE CLINCHERS

Any ghost story, whether real or fictional, needs at least one clinching, transcendent moment. It might occur during the build-up or – better still – as a feature of the final manifestation. Alternatively, this hallmark of ghostliness is earned by no single detail, but by the overall effect of the story. I was about to write that there must be an element of subjectivity about what constitutes a 'clincher', but away with such politesse. I believe that most of us know one when we come across it, because the hairs on the back of our neck do lift. (Or they do whatever Kipling said they do).

Here at any rate are six that worked for me.

1. *Some Homunculi*
In Sheridan Le Fanu's ghost story, 'The Familiar' (1872), Captain Barton, a retired seaman, is tracked by a man who looks like a sailor he once knew and treated badly – only smaller. He consults a doctor, asking: 'Is there any disease, in all the range of human maladies, which would have the effect of perceptibly contracting the stature, and the whole frame – causing the man to shrink in all his proportions, and yet to preserve the exact resemblance to himself in every particular – with the one exception, his height and bulk...?'

It is a brilliant formula for a manifestation: a man who looks as he did in life, but smaller. The homunculus, the compressed human form, has always frightened me, which is why the ending of Nicolas Roeg's film, *Don't Look Now*, has cost me so many hours of sleep. I don't like Mr Punch either. I once knew a Punch and Judy man. He was a big bloke, and he liked a drink. He'd say to me that his shows were 'not suitable for children' and he was only half joking. The climax of one of M.R. James's best ghost stories, 'The Story of a Disappearance and an Appearance' (1919), features a dreamed account of a Punch and Judy show that begins, apparently in a darkened interior, with the single toll of a huge bell. When Mr Punch hits his victims with his stick, there is 'the sound of bone giving way'.

After the final murder, as the stage grows darker, 'Punch came out and sat on the footboard and fanned himself and looked at his shoes, which were bloody, and hung his head on one side, and sniggered in so deadly a fashion that I saw some of those beside me cover their faces...'

It is the violent power that is packed into the small frame that makes the homunculus frightening. Ventriloquists' dummies are frightening because they are small and hard. At least, the ones made out of wood or plastic are hard. The floppy figures are more benign, as are their control-lers. I once attended a ventriloquist's convention, and the vents with the hard figures would intimidate those with the soft ones. The other reason ventriloquists' dummies are frightening is that they speak in voices not their own, like the sybils of Ancient Egypt, or the mediums of the nine-teenth century. The most frightening sequence in the port-manteau ghost film, *Dead of Night* (1945), is the one in

which Michael Redgrave plays a ventriloquist who is possessed by his dummy, and it has been said that this was
inspired by a story of 1931 by Gerald Kersh, 'The
Extraordinarily Horrible Dummy'. In this, the dummy
teaches its master ventriloquism. An onlooker notes that
there was 'something disgustingly avid in the stare of its
bulging blue eyes, the lids of which clicked as it winked.'

Real life ventriloquists do not go out of their way to
distance their craft from necromancy. When I was a boy, a
friend of mine had an *Archie Andrews Annual*. Archie
Andrews was a wooden schoolboy operated by Peter
Brough in – conveniently for Brough who was not a very
good vent technically – a radio series. I remember, as an
eight year old, being appalled by a supposedly amusing
story in the annual, in which Archie Andrews spilled out
of Peter Brough's suitcase at an airport and was seen by
a passing woman who just could not be persuaded that
he wasn't the corpse of a little boy!

2. *The Welsh Egg*

Here is the second story told to my friend David by Ada,
whose story about the ironing ghost has already appeared.
I like it because of the apparent production of proof of a
ghost, just as, in 'Wandering Willie's Tale', Steenie
Steenson comes away from the encounter with the ghost
of Sir Robert Gauntlet holding a receipt in his hand.

My grandfather was Welsh, from Blaenau Ffestiniog.
He emigrated to America in his teens and became a
Congregationalist minister. He died in 1969 and my

nephew, Bryn, saw him in New York in 1981...

My aunt Mary was putting Bryn to bed for a nap; he was four years old at the time. She went to get him and when he woke up, he said, 'I want an egg – the same type of egg that grandfather likes.' My aunt was astonished because he'd never known either of his grandfathers. She asked him, 'What kind of egg?' and he said what sounded like...now let me get this right phonetically...'Oo-ee weddy verwi'. That's the Welsh for soft boiled egg – the spelling would be: wy wedi'i ferwi. My aunt did know some Welsh – which Bryn certainly didn't – and she asked him, 'How do you know about that?' He said, 'Grandfather told me when I was asleep.'

3. *Old Q---*

After co-writing *Phantasms of the Living*, Frank Podmore went solo with another fascinating compendium: *Apparitions and Thought Transference* (1894), and one of the oddest and therefore most compelling of the accounts in the book is listed as 'Number 123' under the heading 'Less Common Forms of Hallucination'. It is recounted by a 'Mr J---', a man 'well known in the scientific world', who had succeeded the late 'Mr Q---' as the librarian of 'X Library'. By way of introduction it is pointed out that Mr J--- had never met or seen his predecessor at the library; he concedes that he may have overheard library assistants describing him, but he has 'no recollection of this'.

Late one evening, Mr J--- was working in the library

(which was in Bracknell in Berkshire) when he looked up to see a face looking round one of the bookcases. 'I say looking round, but it had an odd appearance, as if the body were in the bookcase, as the face came so closely to the edge, and I could see no body.' The face was pallid and hairless; he advanced towards it. 'I saw an old man with high shoulders seem to rotate out of the end of the book-case, and with his back towards me and with a shuffling gait walk rather quickly from the bookcase to the door of a small lavatory.' Mr J--- followed the figure into the lava-tory, and found it empty.

He later mentioned the sighting to a local vicar, who said, 'Why, that's old Q---.' Q---, it turned out, had lost all his hair, including eyebrows, in a gunpowder accident; and he walked with a shuffle.

Frank Podmore rationalised this as a case of thought transference: 'Mr J--- saw the figure of Mr Q--- in the library because some friend of Mr Q---'s was at that moment vividly picturing to himself the late librarian in his old haunts.'

The appealing thing about the story is that it is all of a piece: the slightly undignified elision of man and book-shelf matches the bathetic denouement in the lavatory – and the shuffling walk and the hairless head compliment the overall dowdiness. It has the coherence, in other words, of truth.

4. *The Lusitania Prophecy*
To begin with the facts: the *Lusitania*, which had been

launched in 1906, was sunk off Ireland by a German U-boat on May 7th 1915. It was approaching Liverpool having sailed from New York. The targeting of a civilian vessel stimulated outrage against Germany, and was a factor in America's entry into the Great War.

In *Science and Parascience*, Brian Inglis mentions that before the Great War there had been 'countless portents of a coming Armageddon', mostly 'in vague general terms', but one prediction (although it's not quite that), made 'before the international situation became really serious', catches his eye. It was made by Dame Edith Lyttelton, who was a relation of the above-mentioned Prime Minister and SPR President, Arthur Balfour. Besides being involved in numerous philanthropic activities, Dame Edith was an SPR member herself and a practitioner of automatic writing, which means writing in a trance state while in touch with spirits.

On some date unrecorded, and after the launch of the ship but well before its loss, she transcribed the word 'Lusitania' followed by 'Foam and fire – mest [sic] the funnel.'

What makes this particularly sinister is the horrible compression of the word 'mest', a combination perhaps of 'mast' and 'messed'. It implies a desperate, ham-fisted attempt at communication, an attempt to re-master language by some entity labouring under the inconvenience of being dead.

A boiler exploded as the ship went down, incidentally, causing a funnel to collapse.

5. *The Bideford Dream*

This story was originally told to my friend David by a friend of his called Keith. When Keith heard that I was working on a book about ghosts, he kindly re-told it to me.

This happened thirty years ago on a Saturday, the first lovely day of spring. I was with my first girlfriend, Margaret, and we'd booked to stay at a guest house in Bideford on the coast of Devon. We went up from London in my old mini, a four hour trip from London. When we got to Bideford it was glorious, and I remember the room...Very bright and airy; good double bed, net curtains wafting at the sash windows, which were open a little way to let the breeze in. It had been a long drive, so we decided to have an afternoon sleep, and it's important to bear in mind that I locked the door before we did so. I fell asleep straight away, and I dreamt that someone came into the room. He stood at the window for a while, and he watched me as I lay in bed although I wasn't really aware of his face. It was one of those dreams where you can't do anything, although I seemed to be fine with him being in the room. It was the noise of him closing the door in my dream that woke me up.

Later, we were walking along the beach. I said to Margaret, "You know, I've just had a strange dream." I started describing it to her; she grabbed by arm and said, 'I've just had the same dream' – the closing door had woken her up as well. I was very taken aback but, well...a co-incidence, and that's all there was to it.

That evening we dined in the guest house, and we got talking to a man called Mark. He lived in Surrey, and he was the proud owner of a new Ducati motorbike, which he'd bought a few days before. He was on his way to test it out in Cornwall. He was a lovely bloke, and we spent most of the evening with him. The next morning we woke up a bit late. I was in the bathroom, and I heard the motorbike revving up. I leant out of the window, and waved down at Mark. He waved back, and went off.

We were out all day, and when we came back, the landlady came straight up to us, saying, "We've just had a call from the Cornish police. Mark's been knocked off his motorbike and killed." Apparently he'd had a receipt from the guest house in his pocket. When we'd met him at dinner, we didn't connect him with the figure in the dream. Afterwards, though... it all seemed to link up.

I too think it links up. It doesn't quite fit any of the normal ghost story templates, but makes sense in a ghostly way.

*

I do have a sixth clincher, but I reserve that for my conclusion...

CONCLUSION
Derek Acorah and
the Re-enchantment
of Ipswich
or, *British Ghostliness today* (*continued*)

According to my friend David, ghosts are essentially a 'transcendence of time', and it seems to me that there is a particular market for that quality in our society. In modern Britain, time does not flow very smoothly. Every politician seems to have to promise a revolution. What was Tony Blair's brain-dead slogan: 'Let the change continue'? Ever since the Second World War we've been afflicted by neophilia in the public sphere. Youth is celebrated in our culture to the point where not only do the people the journalists write about have to be young and good looking, but so do the actual journalists.

In the sixties and seventies, out of a need to over-compensate for being so old-fashioned as to have recently possessed an empire, we ruined most of our towns and cities for the sake of the car. We razed, in short, the haunts of our ghosts, against which vandalism there is now a reaction. The planning mistakes of the past are regretted. We know our towns and cities have lost much of their charm; that we have lost a sense of place. At the time of writing the so-called Red Tories want to re-enchant Britain, and certainly Ipswich needs to be re-enchanted. Or something...

I am walking out of the railway station towards the centre of town. I pass a bland football stadium; a sort of Americanised pool hall-cum-bar; an underpass. I come to the heart of the town, where medieval buildings co-exist uneasily with buildings that from their style and character, or lack of it, proclaim themselves retail outlets rather than shops.

I walk past a church, which is closed. But then it is early evening on a weekday and all churches in Britain are closed at that time – and most others. Derek Acorah however, 'without question the number one television psychic in the UK', is open for business and performing tonight at the Regent Theatre.

It's a warm evening, and I have gained the sense, while walking through Ipswich, that most of the population has gone elsewhere. I have this sense still more strongly when entering the theatre lobby. There is certainly no crush; just a few pockets of people: more women than men, a higher than average wearing all black. Derek Acorah himself only wears monotones, and there's a big picture of him on every page of the glossy programme: Derek in a black and white striped 'V' neck jumper and no shirt on underneath; Derek in a white leather jacket; Derek in a pin-striped suit with a black 'T' shirt. The earring is constant. He can get away with all this (just about), by virtue of being a good-looking fifty-nine year old with a lot of apparently phosphorescent hair.

I quote from the beginning of the strangely spaced-out biography appearing in the programme: 'Derek Acorah has been a familiar face on television for over twelve years now. In the days when Derek was conducting one-to-one sittings, initially from a small shop premises in the Wavertree area of Liverpool and then subsequently from his office in Liverpool City Centre, nobody dreamed that the cheerful Scouse medium would one day grace their television screens. Only Derek and one or two noted mediums on the Liverpool circuit knew that the Spirit "had something special" lined up for him. It was Lilian Star who first told him, "I can see your name in lights"...'

His first big break is then described: 'It happened that one day a researcher for Granada Breeze, the satellite arm of Granada Television in Manchester, telephoned Derek. She explained that she worked on a programme called *Livetime*, a daily magazine programme presented by Becky Want. Being National Tea Week the following week, she had the idea that it would be different to invite a psychic on the programme to talk about the reading of tea leaves...'

It will already be apparent that nobody satirises Derek Acorah like Derek Acorah, even if it is done unconsciously in his case.

He walks on stage to the sound of ethereal New Age

music, and a portentous American voiceover (we're in Ipswich, Derek, not Texas) intones 'Welcome to the psychic world of Derek Acorah...As he astounds you with his knowledge of the esoteric.' The only 'set' is a small table with a glass of water on it.

He begins by explaining his credo: 'The most important thing for me is that there is no death, only transference to a place of beauty.' His spirit guide, his 'control' to use the Victorian term, is one Sam, 'My best mate in the spirit world'. He warns us that he will occasionally break off to talk to invisible Sam, and when he does so he bows his head, frowns and perhaps touches his ear. He looks like a man listening to an earpiece, and people with earpieces have high status in modern Britain. TV presenters wear them, and they too must occasionally commune with some invisible higher force, namely their producer. So these moments of intensive communication with Sam, for which he must beg our indulgence, remind us all that Derek is a big star.

'Right,' he says, emerging from one of these conflabs, 'the first lovely spirit to step forward here is a lovely lady, seventy-three, seventy-four, five foot four inches tops, rather a talkative spirit...she's talking now...It wasn't Alzheimers that took her over, it was...unconsciousness.... She's talking of her love for John.'

And so it begins. Derek is heading out into the stalls looking for the audience member for whose sake this spirit has descended into the 'atmosphere'. Meanwhile I'm thinking 'Can you die of unconsciousness?' and 'John is a very common name.' As he prowls the stalls, calling 'I'm getting a name for this lovely lady...I'm getting an Anne. Is there someone here who knows an Anne?' I begin to feel my first twinge of admiration for Acorah. He is completely unembarrassable. Eventually a woman puts up her hand. She 'might' know who he means. 'She's talking about a job that hasn't been done,' reports Derek, and the woman smiles in recognition. 'Is there a job about the house that hasn't been done?' asks Derek. 'Oh yes,' says the woman, laughing. She must be a plant, I decide.

The question of whether or not the audience members who respond to the spirits (which 'step forward' into the atmosphere at the rate of about one every ten minutes) are plants dominates my thinking throughout the first half of the show. If they are plants then they're very good actors, a cut above Acorah as performers. They laugh ruefully at the little insights into their lives; they genuinely go red, and one woman seems to shed a real tear when Acorah says, 'I'm seeing a little baby...oh, very happy, very well cared for...Was a baby lost?' Yes, the woman had had a miscarriage some years before. He says to another woman: 'Is there something...are there lawyers involved?' She pulls a face and nods. But it's all right, since the spirit has had a look at the papers and everything's going to be fine. Derek never gives bad news to anyone; that's not what his gift is for.

He lurches between what seem accurate insights and preposterous generalisations. One spirit, we are informed with an air of great revelation, was so bold in life that he 'moved away from his place of birth.'

Acorah sometimes alludes to poltergeist activity – of a benign sort – in the homes of the people who recognise the spirits. 'This gentleman...when he's come into the atmosphere...He's caused a lot of what we call audible noises.'

Aren't most noises audible – if not all? But his mention of 'knocking sounds near the tv' provokes furious nodding from the audience member.

Was that audience member a stooge though? I take the issue up with some of the punters during the interval. 'Nah,' says one middle-aged man. 'He'd need...what? A dozen every show and they'd have to be different in each theatre. It'd cost him a fortune.' I ask a young woman whether she finds Derek convincing. 'Well, I've had readings done. I do have my own spirit guide, so...yeah.' Most people gave him the benefit of the doubt.

Returning to London on the oddly silent and empty last train to Liverpool Street, I decide I can't quite dismiss Acorah completely. Perhaps he just knows what's likely to be going on in a person's life by their appearance or demographic profile, which is a sort of talent. But then again, I believe that he *believes* he has psychic ability. And he is certainly significant as an index, and possibly a promoter, of supernatural belief.

Before coming to Ipswich I'd spoken by phone to Caroline Watt, senior lecturer in psychology at Edinburgh University, which has the only endowed, and probably the leading, parapsychology unit in Britain. She told me that 'ghost hunting groups are booming' in Britain at the moment, and when I asked why, she cited Derek Acorah's haunted house investigation series, 'Most Haunted'. Not that she was endorsing Acorah. (Another more recent factor, she felt, might be the recession: 'There is evidence that people suffering a lack of control over their environment are more prone to supernatural belief.')

My problem with Acorah, I reflect, as I walk the length of the train in what would prove a futile search for a buffet car, is the problem Anthony Trollope had with the more numerous mediums of his day. He reported in a letter of 1868 that he found the evidences presented at séances, to be 'unworthy of the grand ceremony of death'.

Acorah hadn't frightened me; in fact he'd bored me to the extent that I'd left his show before the end.

Returning to my seat, I decide there can't be more than twenty people on the entire train – and most of them are asleep. According to the research mentioned in my introduction, eight of these would believe in ghosts. Of these eight, possibly one would have *seen* a ghost. (Ten per cent of Britons, we are regularly told, have seen a ghost, but I can't find a source for this).

I suppose it is time for me to admit that I myself have never seen a ghost, and that I must rely on others to do it for me...

One of my very favourite ghost stories is called 'Dead Men Walk' by Alex Hamilton, which I read in a collection called *Scottish Ghost Stories* (2005). In that beautifully droll story a journalist called Smithson is sent to Orkney by his

features editor. At first Smithson objects:

> 'Why not send Flett? He was born there.'
> 'That's why.'
> 'And when I get there?' challenged Smithson.
> 'Mill about in the stuff. Under the skin a bit. Drag in
> some history if you want.'

After a series of charming encounters with Orcadians, Smithson meets a girl with red hair. He tells her that his story is not panning out. 'Perhaps you've been looking too hard,' she says, and she points down to towards the plain, and the Standing Stones of Stenness: 'indecipherably ancient...a wide circle of dolmens, on a slightly raised turf between two tarns.' She tells him that this is the night when those stones are said to move. Smithson says, 'They won't move if I'm looking.' She replies, 'Would you be content if I saw them move?' So he stands with his back to the stones while looking at the girl: 'In her eyes I saw the stones move.' (When, a couple of days later he files his article, the features editor says, 'Most of it's padding.')

The person nearest to me who has had a supernatural experience – or what I consider to be one – is my father. As a teenager he was plagued by a recurring nightmare: 'I would hear the sounds of a mass of people moving past the head of my bed – a constant succession, streaming past with urgent voices I couldn't make out, and... echoing noises, and a whole sort of atmosphere of illness and crisis. I would know when it was coming on, and I would think, "Not again", but I couldn't stop it, and it would carry on even after I woke up: these people moving, always behind my head. I would have to get up and make a cup of tea, and then it would gradually fade away.'

When he was about sixteen, he made a connection with an earlier event. He recalled that, aged five or six, he had once been taken out of his normal bedroom and put to bed in a downstairs room in the family home in Cameron Grove, York. In that room, the bed head was close to the door and beyond that door was the entrance hall to the house. His mother was pregnant at the time with either his younger brother or his younger sister, he now can't recall which. As far as he was concerned at the time, he slept through the night, only to find out in the morning that a complication had occurred in the pregnancy, life-threatening to his mother – to whom he was particularly attached. There had been a crisis. An ambulance and doctors had come, and they had taken his mother to hospital to induce the birth. When he made this connection, the nightmare went away.

This to me is a clincher, as previously defined. It is mysterious; it repays thought, and its ghostliness touches on birth rather than death, creating the disturbing sense that there is little distinction between them.

As I type this, the clock on my laptop shows midnight and my train is drawing into Liverpool Street; I am ready for bed, and I wish my readers goodnight, and sweet dreams.

A GHOST STORY
Little Jack's, or
The Secret Trust

His full name was George Meredith Arthur Blundy but being his clerk I never called him anything except Mr Blundy. Bob Grafton, the Junior Partner, called Mr Blundy Bill, and I never got to the bottom of that one – couldn't see him as a Bill at all, but Bob Grafton had been at Cambridge University with him, so be obviously knew something I didn't.

As someone said of someone, Mr Blundy 'ran on rails'. Into the office at eight, out of it by six; then two whiskies at The Grapes before driving home. (And him one of York's leading solicitors! But I can assure you it was normal behaviour for the seventies). On Wednesdays he went to The Grapes an hour later because he'd go to the Minster beforehand. Evensong. On Friday he'd go an hour earlier because he'd drive off to his place in the country. Also on Friday, he had tea in Betty's Tea Rooms with York's only barrister: Richard Clarke QC – that's if Clarke wasn't in court. If lunch with a client was on the cards, then Mr Blundy would take them to Ristorante Bari, the Italian place in The Shambles, which was just about the best – and in fact the only – restaurant in York at the time.

Mr Blundy was a little chap, wiry like a jockey. He was red-faced, with very blue eyes and wavy grey hair of the sort you don't seem to see these days. As for the redness, I would tell Nelly Drew – the office junior – that was down to the drink, and she would say, 'No, he was in the desert in the war...it's wind burn.' Well, Nelly was a bit in love with him, so that's what was going on there, but if Mr Blundy knew of her feelings, he never took advantage. I remember her telling me, in the Olde Starre Inn, while sipping one of the hundreds of lunchtime rum and blacks I must have bought her in '75 and '76 (because I *was* trying to take advantage of Nelly Drew), 'He's a gentleman of the old school. He never opens his umbrella, you know.'

'What? Not even in the rain?'

'Well,' said Nelly, 'He's hardly going to open it when it's *not* raining, is he? He was an officer in the Guards, and they always keep their umbrellas rolled up.'

'Okay,' I said, rolling a fag. 'Why?'

'Style, I suppose.'

'What do they use their umbrellas *for* then?'

And she'd obviously done her homework, because she came back straight away: 'Hailing taxis.'

I liked hearing that from Nelly Drew – it was the kind of thing I might have told *her.* It comes under the heading of arcania, for which I have a taste.

But nobody hailed a taxi in York. You *booked* a taxi and waited about half an hour for it to come, which Mr Blundy had no need to do. He had a blue Jaguar XJ6 with shift. Old school, you see. Beautiful interior of course, like all Jaguars, but absolutely reeked of cigarette smoke. Mr Blundy smoked Player's Navy Cut – a very strong fag indeed – and when, after knowing him a few months, I plucked up the courage to ask him why, he gave that sudden smile of his that always came as a surprise, and said, 'You know Geoff, I think it may be nothing more than the nautical design of the packet.' Well, everyone smoked in those days. I seem to recall that clients would be offered cigarettes when they came into the office, not that very many did come in. We all worked mainly by telephone, and Mr Blundy wouldn't do much criminal law, which tends to fill a solicitor's office with all the aggrieved relatives and hangers-on of the accused. I once asked him outright why he hardly touched crime, and he said, 'I don't like criminals, Geoff. Do you?' I said, 'But they deserve representation, Mr Blundy.' 'Do you think so?' he said.

Mr Blundy was quite the fascist in some ways, but even though commercial property was the backbone of the business, he'd never act for a developer he thought 'rapacious'. He was also generally very decent to all of us, and a rare exception to the rule that all public school products are treacherous bastards. For example, he was always on at me to take articles. (An articled clerk is a trainee solicitor, or was back in the seventies, whereas a solicitor's clerk was just a solicitor's clerk). I told him I was looking to find a filling station or car showroom to run with my brother – that was always the long-term plan, and I made no secret of it – but Mr Blundy said I had a natural talent for drafting, and he was giving me wills, deeds of trust and statements of claim to draw up from day one. He'd come up to me with a document and say, 'Now Geoff, I *could* give this to Bob, but I want a safe pair of hands on it', and he'd give a wink to Bob Grafton.

Our office was in Little Stonegate, which is a sort of courtyard off Stonegate proper. Stonegate is old, but Little Stonegate is older. I mean, parts of it are *Norman*. Today – I kid you not – it is 'York's Restaurant Quarter', but in Mr Blundy's day it was so many storehouses with blacked up windows and doors that looked as though they weren't meant to be opened ever again. As the light faded on a winter's afternoon, you could barely see across from our offices to the storehouses on the other side; then the lamp in the middle of the court would be illuminated – about four o'clock sort of time – and the buildings opposite would come back in all their complete deadness.

I remember those winter afternoons in the office, and how made-up I used to feel, with a secure job right in the middle of the beautiful ancient City of York. I mean, picture the place in 1976: 360-odd pubs (one for every day of the year, it was said), and about as many churches to counterbalance; dusty little sweetshops, blackened City Walls, diesel engines winding in and out of the dirty great station under the endlessly falling rain. But it was on one of these afternoons – late in '76, when I was 21 years old – that I began to have the first inkling of what life and death are all about.

Bob Grafton was drafting a long will, been at it all day. As usual, he made a soft popping sound as he drew on his pipe. I was working on a simpler will – a Mr Paul Kay of Burton Stone Lane was leaving his house and his stamp collection and not much else, to his two daughters. I was smoking; occasionally reaching out for 'Theobald on Wills', occasionally yawning. (Well, it's better than a sleeping pill is 'Theobald on Wills'). The clock was ticking, the main office fire...well, that ticked too, if it was going right, and it certainly was just then. Outside in the gloomy court, the rain was falling. Mr Blundy was in his office which was not known as 'Mr Blundy's Office', but the 'inner-office', and he made no trouble at all about Bob Grafton using it if Grafton wanted to speak to a client in private. On this occasion, though, Mr Blundy was in there on his own, and the door was shut, which might mean he was about his trusts.

Mr Blundy was a trustee many times over... I suppose because he was trust*worthy*. A trust, putting it crudely, is property given by the settlor to a trustee who holds it for the benefit of a third party: the beneficiary. Usually the settlor is just about to die, and usually the trustee is not paid for the responsibility he takes on. In practice, even in sleepy old York, the beneficiary is very often a chap's mistress, or the child he had fathered by that mistress, and in these cases the trust is usually kept secret for obvious reasons. Hence 'secret trusts'.

Now some secret trusts are more secret than others.

Generally speaking, Mr Blundy would let Bob Grafton in on anything. I admit that *certain* trusts were kept in Mr Blundy's deeds safe when not being worked on, but... well I suppose I'm saying it was unusual to see his door closed.

At four o'clock, Nelly Drew gave me a smile over her typewriter. It wasn't really *for* me though. It meant she could hear through the closed door that Mr Blundy was dictating. The office had just acquired a dictating machine. It was the idea of Bob Grafton who was go-ahead in spite of his pipe, and Mr Blundy had not been keen at first. I heard him say to Bob Grafton, 'You know, I've just got ingrained prejudice against speaking to inanimate objects.' He came round to it eventually though, even if he'd never quite mastered the machine. It was quite a laugh to watch him, and quite a laugh to *think* of him using it, hence the smile from the beautiful Nelly.

Then we heard Mr Blundy's telephone ringing, and the dictation stopped as he took the call. A few minutes later he came out of the inner office looking odd. I don't know quite what it was about him, but Bob Grafton spotted it too, and he took his pipe out of his mouth, sharpish like. Mr Blundy put the tape of his dictation onto Nelly's desk for typing up. He then took his coat off the stand, and turned and nodded to all of us at once, whereas normally he'd have a word for each of us individually at knocking off time. But that's not the point. The point is it *wasn't* knocking-off time. It was barely five o'clock. As he walked out of the door, Bob Grafton looked up and said, 'I say, Bill...' which was the equivalent of somebody shouting at the top of their voice in another kind of office.

When Mr Blundy had gone, Nelly, holding the tape, looked close to tears. Mr Blundy had not said 'Goodnight' to her. Bob Grafton put his pipe on his desk and stood up.

'Has he got anything on tonight, Nell?'

She looked at the office diary, which was always kept open on her desk.

'Nothing.'

I said, 'He's probably going to the post office on his way to The Grapes.'

After a while, Nelly put on her earphones and started typing the dictation. At six, Bob left and Nelly carried on typing. I liked watching her type; I liked watching her do anything. At six twenty-five we were both still in the office, and I thought: this is becoming rather erotic. I should mention that I was something of a Jack-the-Lad back then: feather cut, Chelsea boots, 100 per cent polyester suit with bell-bottomed trousers and lapels that were wider than *me*. (I'm a skinny little bugger, always have been). And now Nelly was looking back my way. I knew she had a bloke in the background but I thought: what's happened with our boss has stirred her up somehow, put her in the mood. Still looking at me, she said, 'Come here' in a really excitingly *rude* way. She was pressing buttons on her tape machine. She took her earphones off as I went over, and passed them to me. 'Listen to this,' she said.

The dictation was just Mr Blundy giving advice to a client about something. Landlord and tenant stuff. Then I heard, on the tape, the ringing of Mr Blundy's phone, and he hadn't knocked the machine off, so I got his end of the phone call, or the first few seconds of it until he realised he was taping himself and switched off the recorder.

'Blundy', said Mr Blundy. (That's how he always answered the phone). Then, 'Hello' (rather short, that). Another pause, and then 'How lovely to hear from you. How are you?' (I thought: he was expecting this call, but he doesn't like the person he's speaking to). Then Mr Blundy said, very slowly: 'But the Morley child has been dead for more than 50 years...*So I don't see how that can be possible.*'

The day after Mr Blundy had started acting oddly, he came into work at eleven looking worn out, and asked Nelly to book ten rooms at the Viking Hotel (the best York had to offer at the time) for a date two weeks hence. They were to be for 'a party from London' and it was all to be done in his name. Then he went into the inner office and shut the door.

Soon after that, I put on my rally jacket, and stepped out into the rain to go and measure a pavement. Personal injury claim against the council, you see. There was always a lot of tripping over in York, probably on account of those 360 pubs and all the cobbled streets. I'd go out with my tape measure, and report that the cobble or paving stone stood proud by an inch and a half. It was always an inch and a half, and the person who'd tripped would get £50 or a hundred if they'd broken a bone, or bugger all if they'd tried the same thing on before.

It was raining when I went in search of my paving slab, which was in Coney Street, just outside the menswear shop: John Collier's. But I was thinking of a different John as I wondered through the busy medieval streets: Mr John Morley, confectioner. When Mr Blundy had spoken of the long-dead 'Morley child', he must have meant the child of John Morley, who himself had died sometime before the last War, and who, I happened to know, had been a friend of Mr Blundy's father. He wasn't on a par with the Rowntrees or the Terrys, the really famous sweetmakers of the city, but I'd seen pictures of him in the York guides and histories that I liked to read: dark, good-looking...evidently a serious-minded chap in a black suit. He didn't look as though he made sweets for a living, somehow.

Morley's Mints – that was the most famous line, the 'core business' as they say today. There were green ones which were peppermint, and white ones which were peppermint as well, not spearmint as you might hope for the sake of a bit of variety. There'd been a few other kids' lines that had come and gone over the years.

The most interesting thing about Morley's was the factory, which was just downriver of the city centre. It was like a great black cliff, and with all the windows black as well. Above the topmost line of windows was written 'Morley's of York' in letters that were illuminated in red at night, and would glow in the rain like a warning sign to those on the other side of the river, Fulford way. Or those red words – the reflection of them – would lie on the surface of the black water at night, as if the river was time flowing on, but 'Morley's of York' remained constant. You'd never get planning permission for a thing like that now. It blocked off a quarter mile of river frontage and cast this great shadow on the houses on the opposite bank. (And I do believe the prices of those houses rocketed when Morley's factory was pulled down in 1981).

Well, I'd measured the paving stone, and was coming back through St Helen's Square when I saw Mr Blundy. I thought: he must be heading for Betty's Tea Rooms, but it wasn't tea time; it wasn't even lunchtime. And he was crossing the Square in the wrong direction for Betty's. I followed him down Blake Street, which runs off the Square; it was absolutely bucketing down by now, and Nelly was right: he didn't put his umbrella up. I was glad to see him sticking to his guns there at least. He turned right at the end of Blake Street and I thought: he's making for the Minster. The Minster bells were ringing in a crazy sort of way, and it seemed as though the sound was drawing him in, but he veered left, and walked up the steps of the church that stands before the Minster: St Wilfred's. That was the Catholic church, and as he walked through the door, the crazy pealing of the Minster bells stopped and was replaced with a steady chiming of a single bell. I stood still in the rain by the war memorial and counted: eleven o'clock.

There didn't seem to be any doubt about it: Mr Blundy had come off his rails.

I walked back to the office, and reported all this to Bob Grafton and Nelly, who had news of her own, which she'd already mentioned to Grafton. A deed box was missing from the deeds safe in the inner office. I asked whether the box had had a label, because they generally do.

'*In re Morley*,' said Bob Grafton.

(Trusts are labelled '*In re...*' meaning 'In the matter of', and after that comes the name of the settlor).

'Who's taken it then?' I asked.

'Bill has,' said Bob Grafton, and I could tell he was shaken, because he never spoke of Mr Blundy as Bill in front of third parties.

I asked him what the objects of that trust were.

'I don't know,' said Bob Grafton, but he was now sucking on his pipe in a way that made me think he meant to find out.

He quit the office soon after, and came back mid-afternoon, by which time Mr Blundy himself still hadn't returned.

Bob Grafton sat on his desk, and told Nelly and me what he'd found out. He'd spoken to Charlie Whittle, an accountant who did work for us; he audited the accounts of some of the trusts, and that gave him knowledge of the secret ones. Now he was a bit of a loose cannon was Charlie Whittle – always getting divorced, and thrown out of golf clubs. He was more like a barrister than an accountant in that respect. His tipple was 'gin and fizz' and that's the kind of chap he was. Over a couple of these at The Grapes he'd told Bob Grafton what he remembered of *In re Morley*. It was quite technical; I was never very well up on trust law anyway and nor, come to that, was Bob Grafton, but this is the gist of what he said.

In re Morley was actually two trusts, created by John Morley of Morley's Mints. There were currently three trustees: 'two chaps from London', according to Charlie Whittle, and Mr Blundy, who'd inherited his trusteeship from his own father, who – as mentioned – had been a good friend of John Morley's, both of them being York aristocracy, so to speak. One trust was for the maintenance in good health and happiness of a certain Mr Saul Chadwick. (Lucky him, I thought.) The beneficiary of the second trust was a club: a 'philosophical society' of some kind. Charlie Whittle – not being a very philosophical sort of bloke himself – had not understood what this involved, and did not see why philosophers needed to do research anyway. But he knew that this club or society had a good amount of money to spend in pursuit of its objects, and that two properties in central York were to be kept at its disposal. They could do with these whatever they wanted, and what they wanted to do with them was *nothing.* They were to be kept empty.

'What properties?' I said.

'Whittle could only remember one,' said Bob Grafton. 'The River House – that big place in Skeldergate.'

'When was the trust made?' I said.

'Whittle couldn't remember.'

'....Because this Chadwick must be getting on. John Morley died before the last War, didn't he?'

Bob Grafton, re-lighting his pipe, was nodding, 'But the trust might have been made in 1939 for all we know – and Chadwick might have been very young at the time.'

[208]

That night after work I walked through the rain, and down the steps off Ouse Bridge that take you into Skeldergate. It was partly out of sheer curiosity, and partly because I felt that if I could crack the mystery of Mr Blundy's odd behaviour that might make Nelly Drew come across. A sordid little scheme, you might think, but I was a randy bugger back then.

Skeldergate...

I tell you, it was *made* for rain that street... Cobbled in those days, with a great gutter down the middle, and close at hand the river, for more supplies of water if necessary. This was central York, but you wouldn't have known it, since it was always deserted. There were a few businesses: a place that sold beds, a place where an old bloke occasionally – when he could be *bothered* – auctioned off old bikes, but they were the sort of places that carry the announcement on the door: 'By Arrangement', 'By Prior Appointment Only'. The street was separated from the river Ouse by some big buildings that had once been warehouses (for cargoes that, even in the Seventies, had been transferred to road long since), and these would generally have derricks sticking out of the front, like great rusty gibbets. There was also the headquarters of the York Sea Cadets, whose building was called the *S.S.*... something or other, and which they pretended was a ship.

And then there was The River House.

I hadn't known it was called The River House, but as soon as Bob Grafton had mentioned the place, I'd recalled that John Morley had lived there. He must have been attached to the river, John Morley, since this place where he'd lived and raised his family was only a little way upstream from his factory. From the river-side, it looked like one of the warehouses, only better kept and without the indignity of a word like 'GRAIN' or 'FLOUR' painted on it in giant letters. I should mention that Skeldergate features in a Wilkie Collins novel, *No Name*, (not *quite* up there with *The Moonstone* if you ask me), and he refers to 'the dingy warehouses and joyless private residences in red brick.' Well 'The River House' was one of the joyless private residences, except that nobody resided there.

Standing in Skeldergate I was looking at the rear of the property. At all the windows were wooden shutters, closed and stripped of paint or varnish. No light came from within. I stepped back from it and looked up at the top windows. I then began to hear a rising whistling noise, which I thought it might be the Sea Cadets a few doors along, because they did go in for whistling, piping each other aboard their warehouse-cum-ocean-going vessel. But this was not the night for the Sea Cadets; their building was silent and dark. Becalmed.

The whistling carried on – now with another sound beginning to rumble underneath it, and I felt very... I think the word is 'vulnerable' standing there in the rain in Skeldergate listening, but I knew I had to wait for whatever came next. When the next thing started I took a single deep breath and stepped back. The River House was going to burst; it had to. Hundreds... No, thousands of tons of water were cascading through it. Not that there was any

sign of water on the outside. There was no leakage what-
soever, but for thirty seconds I stood in front of that house
and heard water falling within it. When the noise stopped I
was somehow released, and I turned away and walked fast
out of Skeldergate and up Micklegate with the feeling that
anything could happen at any time. On my way up Micklegate, I clattered into a milk bottle; it spun on the slimy
pavement, and I thought: 'It's going to bloody stand up
again of its own accord...It bloody *is*!' And I couldn't look
back at it, just in case. I was running by the time I hit the
doorway of the The Kestrel pub, and when I walked up to
the bar, I said 'Hello, good evening, how are you?' to the
landlord which was an attempt to prove everything was
normal, and which of course proved the exact opposite. I
was what they call 'badly shaken', and I *was* shaking too.
If somebody had said to me that common phrase (which I
have never heard anybody say to anybody), 'You look like
you could use a drink', they would have been right, and I
set about some pints of John Smith's, while rolling fag after
fag and playing Rolling Stones records on the juke box.

The following day, Mr Blundy spent longer than normal on the telephone with his door closed, but by mid-
afternoon, Bob Grafton's pipe was back to making its con-
tended popping noise as he and I drew up a couple of
statements of claim. At knocking off time, I asked Nelly
if she'd like to come down to Skeldergate and look at The
River House. She said yes, after a bit of thought. My courage had returned, you see, and I was sticking to my strategy of trying to draw Nelly into the adventure.

It was a fine night, but cold. As we walked along Coney Street, our voices echoed off the fronts of the closed shops, and I could see that Nelly was feeling self-conscious about being out with me even though I'd billed this as an investigation of strange phenomena rather than anything more romantic. Either way, I was feeling a bit lightheaded, and as we walked past Woolworth's, I said: 'You know, the George Inn used to be on this spot. The Bronte sisters stayed here.' Nelly smiled, like somebody being polite to an idiot. Well, I was in unchartered waters now. I was on an after-work date with Nelly Drew.

It was a funny place for it, mind you: Skeldergate: all shadows and more like a sluice than a street. As we walked along it, I could see the river – a black moving road – in the gaps between the houses. We took up position before The River House, and I let Nelly in on what I'd heard the night before, having only given her a rough idea until then. As I spoke to her, I was thinking about how women, when they fancy you, give you serious looks because they're wondering what it might be like to spend their whole future with you. They don't frown at you, with a look as if to say, 'What the hell are you on about?' which was the way that Nelly often looked at me, and the way she was looking at me now. But then she very unexpectedly complimented me.

'You're sensitive,' she said.

'Yeah,' I said, 'That has often been said.'

'Has it? Who by?'

'Certain...people.'

'Come off it,' said Nelly.

I eyed her.

'So now you're saying I'm not sensitive.'

'I mean... *psychic*.'

'Oh,' I said, 'how do you know?'

'I *don't* know. But it looks like it. Have you ever had any similar experiences?'

'One, yes. When I was a kid. Have you?'

'My grandfather,' she said, and she folded her arms and looked down before adding, 'Possibly...I've felt his presence.'

'He's dead is he, your granddad?'

'There's no need to sound so enthusiastic about it.'

We were both looking at The River House.

She said, 'Tell me about when it happened before?'

'I was on holiday at Blackpool,' I said, lighting up a rollie, 'and we were staying at this guest house on the front. At home – and usually on holiday as well – I shared a room with my brother. But this time, me and our kid were to have our own rooms. Well, that was a big treat but when I saw mine I wasn't so keen. It had this off-white wallpaper that was blistered, as though something was trying to come through the bloody wall. There wasn't much in the room except this very high bed right in the middle, with a string hanging down directly above the pillow. That was the light switch. Now, the moment I entered this room I decided it was both empty and full – full of a lot of people who'd spent a holiday in it and then died. Are you with me?'

'Go on,' said Nelly.

'The first night I was lying in bed watching this cord

swinging about two feet above my face because of the draft from the window. I said, "Show me" when the cord was on the upswing, and it stopped. It was held there for about a second; then it carried on swinging. I was eight years old or so.'

'Were you scared?' said Nelly.

'I was,' I said, flicking my rollie into the Skeldergate gutter, 'but not very. I mean, it would be quite depressing if things like that could never happen, don't you think?'

We'd turned away from The River House now, and were facing each other. I could see exactly what she was thinking: that's rather a good story of his; I agree with the moral he's drawn, and I might have to do something about it, like kiss him.

Unfortunately, rather than do that, she said, 'Geoff, you should know that I have a boyfriend and we're going to get married later this year.' I do believe the matter had been in the balance for a moment, and that it might have been again if I'd had the gumption to speak up.

The next day, Mr Blundy asked Nelly to postpone the mass-booking at the Viking Hotel until the 11th of the following month, which would be the 11th of *November*. He also told us we'd be taking on an articled clerk: his own son, Marcus.

Marcus Blundy was the same age as me, but he'd been to St Peter's School, York, the 'Eton of the North', and did not appear to be an exception to the rule about public school people. He had longer hair than me, wider flares, and whereas I had £10 in Luncheon Vouchers every week he had £15, and he called Nelly 'Nell' as if he'd known her for years. It wasn't that his dad indulged him, and Mr Blundy twice stepped in when Marcus tried to get me to draw up affidavits for him on the grounds that he himself had more important things to be getting on with. But Mr Blundy was spending less and less time in the office and more and more in The Grapes. It wasn't until after the events at The River House on November 11th, however, that I thought: we've lost the old Mr Blundy for good.

It was raining in Skeldergate at seven o'clock on that night. I was pacing the street in my rally jacket with collar up and fag on the go, keeping a sort of vigil.

Mr Blundy hadn't been in the office all day. At five o'clock, Bob Grafton had come up to me and – whispering so's not to let Marcus Blundy hear – said, 'It's the night of the hotel booking. I reckon it's connected to the Morley trust.' I said, 'I know' on both counts. He said he was minded to see whether anything might occur in The River House, since that was one of the properties mentioned in the trust, and I told him I'd been wondering the same thing. He said, 'Would you go along and take a look? I'd do it myself only I've a Law Society function in Leeds that I can't get out of.' I told him I'd been thinking of going anyway, so there you are: a true meeting of minds. Nelly was now out of the picture, which bothered me more than I'd expected. But I was still curious, and what had happened with Nelly made me feel reckless into the bargain. Well, I was entitled. Everyone *around* me was rocking the boat, so I thought I'd get in on the action.

The river was moving fast that night, as if it very determinedly following a fixed intention. It was rising too, coming up the slip roads that ran between the houses on that side of Skeldergate. The Sea Cadets weren't about. Nobody was about. At seven-thirty or so, a woman came clattering along the central gutter of Skeldergate wheeling a kid in a pushchair. He was about two and a half, but sat crossed legged like an intelligent middle-aged man. He looked very languid even though soaked, and his mother wheeled him past me, the kid said, 'Why is the river like that, do you think?' His mother replied, 'Because it's rained and rained and rained and rained and....' And she kept saying that until they disappeared into the darkness towards Ouse Bridge.

It was at about five to eight, and I was setting about another roll-up in the shadowy doorway of the bike auction place, that the cars began to arrive, parking either side of The River House. First came two black Ford Granadas – the stylish, streamlined ones, not the boxy models that came later; then Mr Blundy's Jag pulled up, and him in it. A few seconds later came a still better Jag: a black XJS, successor to the E-Type (under the bonnet, the best twin-cam ever to come out of Coventry), and the number plate was personalised, which you didn't so much in those days: MOR 1EY. Out of this stepped a good-looking couple, both very sleek and dark, like their car. The man could have been the son or, more likely, the grandson of John

Morley, and I recalled that the surviving family members had walked away loaded from the sale of the business to some outfit who'd shifted production abroad.

But even the XJS was trumped by the next motor: a black Rolls Royce Phantom *Limousine* – the kind of thing the Queen rides around in. It was customised at the back, so that the rear doors were taller than they otherwise would have been. I thought: What is this? The bloody Earl's Court Motor Show?

The door of the River House opened, so there'd evidently been someone in it all along. Mr Blundy was glad-handing everybody, looking not at all like himself, but too eager to please – and nervous with it. It seemed to be the job of some men in black suits to hold black umbrellas over the more important members of the party, and under these umbrellas, things were being carried into the house: paperwork – some ledgers and files; photography equipment, shining silver flasks. I heard the man at the door greeting his visitors by name. I heard 'Dr Duggan' (this was a woman), 'Professor...' somebody or other. The glamorous couple got a deep nod – more of a bow – and, 'Good evening Mr Morley...Mrs Morley...'

I then noticed that the umbrellas were congregating around the rear door of the Limo. It opened and there sat a creature – all right then, a man – so old that he seemed to have gone round the clock and become young again. I saw a small baby's head coming out forwards from the great bulk of a hunched-back that seemed to be propped directly on top of two shaking, bandy legs. He wore a black double-breasted pin-striped suit, and it slowly came to me as he emerged from the car: he is beautifully dressed. He was smiling as he found his footing in Skeldergate, and I thought: this old boy's happy just to be alive. He moved three paces from the car with some assistance from the umbrella men. He then remained absolutely motionless for ten seconds or so, and the umbrella men were very good about it, very patient, since they too stood stock still. I could then see from the trembling of his mouth, that he was about to smile again, and also to speak. His voice, when it came, was quite firm: posh-northern.

He said, 'Let's...see...whether...we...can't...meet...our... young...friend...halfway.'

The umbrella men smiled at one another. It was a joke of sorts, but evidently not a very good one, even if you knew what he was talking about. Within five minutes, the umbrella men had got him through the front door of The River House, which was then slammed shut, and I was back to square one except for the 50 grand's worth of cars standing outside being rained on. I listened to the distant traffic of York for a while (I was in a state of shock, I suppose) when the front door of The River House was opened once again by somebody who was talking to someone else just inside the door. This time, there being nobody in the way, I could see in.

A wooden staircase lead directly up from the front door, all bare with no carpet and not even any varnish on the wood. Many candles were burning on every stair. A man came out of the door, which was pushed to behind him. He was making for the Limo. When he got there, he opened the rear door and took out two pressurised black cylinders, each about the size of a Thermos Flask. I thought: oxygen? The man returned to the house, tapped on the door, and it was opened for him. He went in, and the door closed once more, but quietly.

Standing in my doorway, I said to myself, 'They didn't slam it.'

I waited two minutes; then I crossed Skeldergate towards The River House, and I knew what I was doing: I was compensating for not having been a man with Nelly Drew. I pushed the door, and it opened, but just then a gust of wind came, and the candle flames all bowed to the right. At first this looked like disaster – it was the most frightening thing that had happened so far – but as I pulled the door to behind me, the flames settled back to the vertical, so that they were now pointing the way upstairs. I saw a tape recorder among the candles on the fourth stair up, and another half a dozen steps beyond that. The spools were still turning, so the creaking of my boots as I walked up was being recorded, and possibly also the beating of my heart, but there was nothing to be done do about that. The reels turned completely silently, I noticed, and you only get that with the top-of-the-range models. But at the same time they were more than that: beautiful somehow, and all of a piece with the house and the candles.

The landing was a wooden corridor, the floor covered with candles, and more tape recorders. I heard low voices to the right. I came to the closed door of what might have been the main room in the house. It would overlook the river. From inside I could hear a fast low muttering: somebody saying, 'The temperature of the room at twenty hundred hours' and the sound of particularly fast typing – a sound I knew from attending court: they had a stenographer in there keeping a record. I heard somebody say, 'Mr Chadwick, are you quite comfortable?' Well, the old boy was Chadwick: the one being preserved by the first of the Morley trusts. I thought that it was either doing a very good job of that, or a very bad one. It was him who spoke next, and his voice was stronger now; all other sounds in the room stopped as he said:

'Master...Young Master...Morley...'

And then his voice cracked, and broke into a sort of really delighted laughter, or perhaps pure amazement. 'I am so happy that you have come in...'

I heard a scream – one of the women; then a very loud and un-ladylike thud; then the sound of concerned male voices. I thought: she's bloody fainted. But Chadwick was carrying on regardless. He said, 'Tell us your impressions of our city of York – your city – after all this time, Master Morley.'

The waterfall sound came. It stopped abruptly and a boy's voice – posh northern – was all that remained, and it was saying, 'The motors cars in the streets...' and then, in a sort of very rapid whisper, 'Criss-cross criss-cross, criss-cross criss-cross.'

A new voice, a man's – not Chadwick's – said, 'Many more than when you were...here', at which yet another voice said, 'Please... Mr Chadwick only will speak to the child.'

Through the door, I could hear somebody crying – one of the women.

Chadwick was saying, 'Please, a little...' and then a hissing noise. Was that the oxygen?

The singing noise came again, and the boy's voice: 'Chimneys...but no smoke...no smoke...no smoke...Open the door.'

And those last words caused a sort of flurry in the room.

'Open the door,' said the boy's voice again.

I would say that I was experiencing all this time a feeling a falling – of racing towards some unknown destination at uncontrollable speed. I looked along the corridor at the candles. Was I meant to open the door? I put my hand to the handle. I withdrew it, since it seemed to me that the boy was telling *them* to open the door in order to reveal me. I was not having that, and I was down the stairs and out of the door.

I never did tell Bob Grafton what happened in The River House. Well, he never asked – not properly. The reason was that first thing the very next day, he had a row with Marcus Blundy over the drawing up of a lease. He spent the morning in the office moaning at Mr Blundy ('But *Bill*...' I kept hearing him say, through the closed door), then he went home. A couple of days later, he came up to me and said, 'Oh yes, about The River House', and I told him I'd seen some sort of social event in there, which was only half a lie. It seemed too big a thing to tell him what I'd *actually* seen, and I couldn't tell Nelly either. It seemed to me that I had lost her. She and her bloke had started viewing show houses on the new estate at Dunnington.

A couple of days after the revelation of The River House, and still dazed by the whole thing, I went to the reference section of York Library and asked for the 'Morley's Mints' file. There wasn't much of it, and I wondered whether one of the shadowy lot connected with *In Re Morley* had made off with half the papers.

What remained was a picture of the factory dated 1925 and proudly labelled 'Taken From The Air'. Well, it was no prettier from the air than it had been from the ground. There was also a brief *Yorkshire Evening Press* interview with John Morley himself from about the same time. He was 'proud to be associated with the city of York' and 'looking forward to expansion in the future'. In the file, unconnected to that article, was a picture of Morley wearing evening dress standing outside what looked to be the Mansion House in York. Alongside him was a much younger woman, dark haired and a real looker. The caption read: 'Mr and Mrs John Morley arrive for the Lord Mayor's luncheon.'

The information I'd been looking for, however, came in some pages cut from a children's magazine of the 1960s called *Get To Know*. The thrilling theme of this particular issue was '*Get to know...York*', and, in among all the usual stuff about the City Walls and the Minster, the writer had for some reason gone to town on Morley's Mints, setting out a long series of facts on the firm, all beginning 'Did you know...?'

Did you know...Morley's factory, on the banks of the river Ouse, is the tallest building in York.

Did you know...The founder of the firm, Mr John Morley, was very interested in research into the paranormal. (In other words, ghosts!)

Did you know...The face on the packets of the mints called 'Little Jack's – which were very popular with children when your grandfather was young – was that of Mr John Morley's own son. This little boy was christened John like his father, but known to all his family as Jack. (Turn to page 15 to see a picture of one of these packets).

Did you know...Little Jack Morley was one of three brothers. He was a very brilliant boy. He sang solos in the Minster choir, and he was too clever for the York schools! (So he was taught privately by a retired headmaster living in Blake Street). But his story is a sad one. The house in which he lived with his family overlooked the river Ouse. One stormy winter's day in 1922, he fell from a second floor window into the river below. Or did this strange little boy jump? He had been quite alone in the room, and the nanny looking after him swore in a court of law that the window had been firmly shut, and that it must have been opened from the inside.

I turned to page fifteen, which was stapled to the others. There was a picture of a 'packet' of Little Jack's, only it wasn't a packet, but a blue tin about an inch and a half square and a quarter inch high. Little Jack's really must have been little. On the lid was a detailed painting of a blonde boy with curly hair; his tongue was sticking out, and on it was a little round sweet like a pill. Underneath (in red) ran the slogan 'Stick to…Little Jack's'. The boy had managed to stick his tongue out without looking at all rude. 'Angelic' would be the word for him. Another would have been 'annoying'. But there'd evidently been a lot more to this kid than met the eye.

Returning the file to the librarian, it struck me that I didn't *believe* the Morley factory had been the tallest building in York. It couldn't have been as high as the main tower of York Minster: two hundred feet. Anyway, next I asked the librarian for books on the paranormal. He showed me to a shelf, and (this being York) it was all the *Yorkshire* paranormal, local ghosts. 'Chadwick' appeared in the index of only one of the titles, which was more of a pamphlet than a book, and called 'The Psychic Circles of the North, 1910-1950'. 'Interest in spiritualism began to decline in the early 1920's,' I read, 'but those two indefatigable investigators, Hart and Meadows, were favourably impressed by a number of young mediums operating in the region at the time, most particularly Saul Chadwick, whose Sunday evening sittings in a large house outside Leeds were the talk of the psychical circles.'

And there was a photograph of the man from those days. He wore a wide-brimmed hat, but even so, you could see he had a ton of black hair. He had a black goatee beard, and held his hand up to the side of his head, as though he had a bad headache but was putting a brave face on it. This was no doubt his 'seeing beyond the veil' expression... and yet it appeared that Chadwick was, as the kiddies say today, 'the real deal'. When I handed the pamphlet back to the librarian (because you weren't trusted to re-shelve it in the right place yourself), he said, 'Find what you were looking for?'

Well, my reading had set a film spooling in my mind: John Morley and his young wife holding séances to contact the dead boy...Darkness and rain falling beyond the window...Chadwick turns up at the door, holding a black umbrella and looking like something in-between an actor and funeral director...But he delivers the goods: he goes into his trance and against all expectation conjures up the brilliant child....On his death bed, Morley calls in Mr Blundy Senior and sets up the trust to look after Chadwick. Why? For the wife, so that *she* could keep in touch with the boy. I just knew that somehow.

But there was another reason as well.

I'll now come up to date, or at least to Wednesday last. But first I'd better say how the firm of Blundy as I knew it fell apart, and what happened as a result.

In March 1977, a few months after my experience in The River House, Nelly Drew quit to get married. She and her husband (an absolute tosser from Heslington) would be honeymooning on a safari in Kenya and then running a sub-post office near Clifton Green. Bob Grafton left at about the same time because he couldn't get on with Marcus Blundy – he found him far too pushy. A few weeks later, Mr Blundy was drunk in the office at nine o'clock in the morning. He put his arm around me, asking 'How old are you, Geoff?' 'Twenty-two, Mr Blundy,' I said. 'You've got it all before you, love,' he said, 'you've got it all before you.' Marcus had to take him home, and his old man was into semi-retirement from then on. I'm sure what he'd seen behind that closed door in The River House had tipped him over the edge, this even though he'd known what he was in for – had done ever since that original phone call. (Although why *that* had shocked him so much I couldn't figure out. Despite being a trustee, he must not have had a full understanding of the purpose of *In Re Morley* until then). I was rather jealous of whatever he'd experienced in that room at The River House; I also thought he should have been able to handle it. Then again, he had certainly taken it *seriously*, and that was to his credit.

After he left the office, I had to rely on rumours and gossip for news of him. I heard that he did eventually convert to Catholicism; that he gave up the drink and was back on an even keel when he died, which he managed to do at midnight on the last day of 1999.

The New Millennium?

Quite honestly, I preferred the old one.

I'd left the firm not long after Bob Grafton, and I bought a filling station off Micklegate with my brother Dave. It hit serious trouble late in 2000, and finally closed on August 14th 2002 (four months ago at the time of writing), not that many people had ever noticed it had been open. One thing we could have done without... the Council kept pedestrianising the bloody streets in the area. It was like one of those puzzles in a kid's comic: 'Trace a line to show how Mr Bloggs the motorist can get to Geoff and Dave's filling station'. And if they couldn't pedestrianise a street near us, then they'd make it one way. I tell you, it's only a matter of time before York Council brings in streets that are pedestrianised *and* one way – that's the ideal they're working towards. I used to wonder: is it revenge for all those actions I'd brought against them over their wonky paving stones? At about the same time I broke up with my latest girlfriend, Marina. Her name alone meant trouble, of course. She'd been a sort of experiment: I thought I'd try going out with someone I didn't much like, on the grounds that it couldn't be worse than all those times I'd hooked up with someone I was genuinely keen on.

In all this time The River House remained unoccupied. I knew that much but didn't often think of it, although one winter's night in the mid-eighties I stopped and stared at five black people carriers turning out of Skeldergate on to Ouse Bridge. A couple of weeks later, I thought I saw the same convoy hogging all the parking spaces on the corner of St Helen's Square and Blake Street, and I recalled that Little Jack had been educated in Blake Street. That all set me wondering about the second of the properties kept empty by the trust. Blake Street was a good address: eighteenth Century, elegant, discreet, bang in the middle of York and busy on a working day, with civilised kinds of shops on the ground floors of the buildings, but the flats above... Some of them did seem permanently dark, and the place echoed to the bells of the Minster, which was just around the corner. It seemed a good compliment to Skeldergate. I never heard the water falling in Blake Street, but it's not far from the river, and it's amazing what trying to control the finances of a collapsing business can distract you from investigating.

After the business went under the situation changed, and I became attuned to the possibilities. I kept Blake Street in the back of my mind, but my main focus was Skeldergate. I took to drinking in the pubs around Bishophill, only a couple of hundred yards up the hill from there. My favourite of these is the The Sun in Splendour, a very dark little pub oddly enough, and quiet. It does have electronic screens in the public bar, but there's usually nothing on them except a few strobing lines and the words 'No Media Detected' (thank Christ). It's part of old York, the shadowy place I loved; and I was now beginning to think of The River House as part of that world, and as the last of the good things in my life rather than the first of the bad ones.

After a couple of Guinnesses and a read of a paperback, I'll light up a rollie (I have also not given up suede jackets and longish hair) and descend along gloomy Fetter Lane into Skeldergate, where I'll stand in front of The River House. I've not heard the whistling or the water falling again, but I feel there's a great potential there, and in these moments the idea that anything called a 'filling station' caused me so much bother seems incredible.

And so we come to early evening, Wednesday last.

I was walking through Rowntrees Park, which lies a little way downstream of Skeldergate. Darkness was falling fast, and the park keeper was striding about ringing a bell like a sort of medieval lunatic. It was closing time in the park, which overlooks the river at about the spot where the Morley's factory was located. As I made towards the gates, I kept having the idea of a life-sized but *lightweight* version the factory being manipulated on the horizon, like a vast black stage flat being experimented with and held at odd angles. I knew from this to go to Skeldergate, and when I got there I also knew to walk down the slip road that ran by the side of The River House. In the seventies, this just led straight down into the water; today, we Council Tax payers have funded signs reading: 'You are now approaching the water's edge', or 'Warning: This is A River', and suchlike. To the left of these is a stone ledge separating the front of the River House from the water – a place where boats might once have moored. I stepped onto this.

The wind flying off the black river made my perch precarious and, as I looked up, the great house seemed to tilt towards me, but its eyes were blind, all the window shutters being closed. 'Show me,' I said, and a slight grating noise started up from the second storey, like something unwinding. The closed shutters there moved inwards, as though being sucked into the house, and after trembling at that point for a count of five seconds, they burst open, smashing against the brickwork on either side and swinging half closed again. Breathing hard – both shocked and not shocked – I edged back along to the slip road, thinking: that was the room in which Chadwick had done his stuff. It was the room from which Little Jack had leapt.

Why?

I walked fast, a little wobbly, up the steps to Ouse Bridge, and it was a relief to see traffic, and then I saw something better: Nelly Drew coming over the bridge. I stood still and watched her approach. How very clever of you, I thought, watching her, to have remained so beautiful after twenty-five years. Of course, I had seen her around town since our days under Mr Blundy, so I knew it anyway really.

She smiled when she saw me, coming out with a lovely, 'Hello stranger', but as she drew nearer, she stopped smiling, and said, 'I hear you've gone...'

'Now you've rather backed yourself into a corner with that one haven't you?' I said, because I was hyper from The River House. 'I've been declared bankrupt, yes, but Walt Disney went bankrupt three times before he built Disneyland. As it happens, I'm working on a similar project myself, so it's a very good omen...What do you think about lunch tomorrow?' I added, still being hyper, and knowing very well that she was divorced from her sub-postmaster.

'All right,' she said, slowly. 'Where do you want to meet?' But this she answered herself, and in a way I liked: 'The

Danish Kitchen?' she said, adding in a charming way, 'On High Ousegate?'

How the Danish Kitchen has not become Costa Coffee, I do not know. It is – like my haircut, I suppose – a survivor of seventies York, and I felt that Nelly had chosen it as a symbol of the days when she and I had been (nearly) together.

The next day, sitting opposite one another on the green banquette seats of the Danish Kitchen on High Ousegate, where the sandwiches come open-topped (well, it's the authentic Danish way), Nelly told me she did a bit of part-time clerical work for Marcus Blundy.

'What car does he drive? Don't tell me, a Subaru Impreza.'

'What's that?'

'It's a bit like a Mitsubishi Evo.'

Nelly folded her arms and gave me her shrewd look, as if to say: well you haven't changed at all. But it wasn't the *frowning* look, and I noticed that she kept turning sidelong, to show me the few grey hairs near her ear, as if to say: 'Do you mind?'

When we'd finished our sandwiches, she sat back in a reminiscing mood, saying, 'You and your psychic experiences...'

Since she'd brought up the subject, and to keep her in the Danish Kitchen, I told her about that momentous night in The River House all those years before, and then filled her in on the latest instalments. When I'd finished – by which time we were standing *outside* the Danish Kitchen

– she said, 'You have a real talent, Geoff. You're lucky.'

'But I'm bankrupt, as you were anxious to point out.'

'I should think plenty of psychics have been that,' she said, and I thought: Yes, that's obviously true, and I pictured a gallery of theatrically dressed fraudsters, all attempting the same far-seeing expressions.

...But then there was ancient Saul Chadwick with his army of umbrella men, his customised Rolls, and the funds of *In Re Morley* behind him. He must be good at his job, just as I'd been good at mine in the days of Mr Blundy but not since. Compared to Chadwick's production in The River House that night, I'd only generated a few flickering indications of the continuing presence in York of Little Jack. I said something of this to Nellie, and she was about to reply as I rolled up a cigarette. Exactly as I struck the match, the Christmas fairy lights strung along High Ousegate were all illuminated, and the co-incidence made Nelly laugh out loud, and forget whatever she was going to say.

As we set off down High Ousegate, Nelly had what was evidently a new thought, and not connected to what she'd been about to say when I struck the match. She said, 'What are we going to do about your financial situation, Geoff?'

A question full of promise, I thought.

Two days later, Marcus Blundy phoned me. Immediately on picking up, I told him I knew what had happened; that

Nelly Drew had suggested he call and offer me work. I told him thanks very much but I wasn't looking to go back to a solicitor's office.

'Hold on,' he said, 'I've got to take a call on the other line.'

So he was keeping me waiting before I could put the phone down on him – that's the public school man all over. When he came back on, he said, 'That's not it. I did see Nelly Drew, and while she was discretion itself, she did let slip something about you....'

There was a pause, both on his side and mine.

'Oh,' I said, 'The Morley business.'

'Can we meet?' he said.

I knew he must have taken over his father's trustee-ship, and I wondered whether he'd decided I knew too much. Perhaps he was going to do me in. But I knew that couldn't be the plan when he said, 'How about Betty's Tea Rooms?'

As the light fades on an afternoon close to Christmas, Betty's Tea Rooms is the place to be. Well, perhaps not for the bankrupt.

Betty's, which opened in 1920, is traditional in style – all except the prices. The prices are what you might call bang up to date. The cakes come on cake stands, and the waitresses wear lacy caps like doilies on their heads. Even a plate of fish and chips is genteel in Betty's. It comes with about four chips (very nice, big ones, mind), a fish knife and a slice of lemon in a sort of silver hairgrip.

The place was packed out – the County set mainly: lawyers, farmers and businessmen, products of the Etons of the North. I took my seat at a window table looking out on to St Helen's Square, which is beautiful, and where 'God Rest Ye Merry Gentlemen' was being played on a species of giant music box superintended by two men in Georgian outfits. This machine is called The York Chimer, and has been a feature of the York Christmas for a hundred years or more. It resembles a highly ornate miniature cathedral on wheels with a mixing handle at the side. The chimer is operated by the members of a York charity who wear the above-mentioned fancy dress and collect donations from the public for the aid of...Well, as I was trying to recall that particular piece of arcania, Marcus Blundy turned up, half an hour late, and talking into his mobile phone.

'Not managed to order?' he said.

Sitting down opposite me, with his back to the window, he was obviously thinking: I'm not surprised. The bent paperback and disposable lighter on the table before me struck a jarring note in this setting of buxom waitresses, chandeliers and Christmas trees.

'Tea?' Blundy said.

'Suits me,' I said.

He was beginning to go a bit red like his father, but that might just have been the cold. He looked rich; he probably *would* drive a Jag, but he wasn't stylish like his dad. He was still at his mobile phone, possibly sending a text message, or at any rate pressing the buttons in a bloody annoying way.

'What I'd like to know,' I said after watching him for a while, 'is how old was the medium, Saul Chadwick?'

Without looking up, Blundy said: 'You say "was".'

'He must dead by now.'

'Correct.' Still tapping away, not looking up. 'He died in '88.'

'Well,' I repeated, 'how old was he?'

'You don't want to know how old he was,' said Blundy.

'You're a trustee now, I suppose,' I said.

He nodded and, still playing with his phone, he answered my earlier question.

'Chadwick died aged at least 109, nobody's quite sure exactly. That's what the best medical care money can buy will do for you; and a strong constitution; and the mountain air. He was at a clinic in Switzerland in his last years. The trust in his favour has naturally lapsed, but the other element of *In re Morley* carries on.'

'The part to do with the philosophical society.'

'Right again.' And, finally putting down his mobile phone, Blundy said, 'How much do you know about it all?'

I told him everything I knew, and everything I'd experienced in and around The River House... Because what did I have to lose?

'You feel you're in psychic communication with the boy?' said Blundy, and he'd picked a bad time to ask that question, because just then the fat party at the next table were taking delivery of half a dozen knickerbocker glories, and the fat *boy* was actually rubbing his hands with delight. I'd never seen anyone do that before.

'I suppose so,' I said to Blundy.

'And what's it like? This feeling.'

I thought: he's a trustee of *In re Morley*, but he's a sceptic.

'You know when you're walking down the street, and you think you're going to meet someone you like, or don't like? And then you do.'

'And when you have this feeling about the boy: Little Jack...Is it the feeling of being about to meet someone you like or someone you don't like?'

I eyed him for a while, because it was a good question.

'Somewhere in-between,' I said. 'It's excitement. A sense of...'

'What?' said Blundy, and he wasn't going to let me off the hook.

'Infinite possibility.'

'Well, that must be a good thing,' said Blundy.

'Yeah,' I said, nodding slowly. 'It's a bit daunting that's all.' He was watching me, because he could see there was more to come. 'It's to do with time not mattering. I mean, you might have wasted 25 years of your life, but you realise that's nothing really. Time is sort of... incidental, overrated.'

Blundy put his hand up, and a waitress came immediately.

'Bottle of champagne and two glasses,' he said; then, to me, 'Changed my mind about the tea at the last minute.'

He didn't ask if I minded, but then again, I didn't.

'You're a sceptic,' I said. 'Why did you take on the trust? What's in it for you?'

He frowned at me.

'Fiduciary duty,' he said. 'The duty of the trustee.'

'I know what it means,' I said.

'You wouldn't have asked my old man that, would you? Your old man didn't put his umbrella up when it was raining.'

'How do you mean?'

'He was old school.'

A light rain was falling beyond the window; a sparkling, Christmassy rain whirling under the soft street lights.

'I've heard the recording of the séance in '76,' said Morley. 'Your footsteps... You really legged it out of there, didn't you?'

'Can you blame me?' I said. 'I mean you'll have heard the boy's voice on the recording, and... Were there photographs?'

He shook his head, pouring champagne into my glass. 'None that came out right. The recording's indistinct as well. But my dad was there – it was the first time he'd gone to a séance, the first time he really had to face what the trust was about – and he was sure he'd experienced something. I mean he was sure to the point of a nervous breakdown. I *wasn't* there, and so I have to rely on second hand accounts... which do vary.' He was pouring champagne into his own glass, as he continued: 'It strikes me that there are three possibilities. No, *four*. Number one: Chadwick was a genuine medium and he raised the ghost of the boy. Two: Chadwick was a fraud, and it was all trickery. Three: You are a genuine psychic and the boy came for you.'

'Hence "Open the door",' I said, drinking champagne.

'Some people do say that was said, or something like it. Yes.'

'What's number four?'

'It's all subjective. Mass hallucination.'

I sat back. It had never occurred to me that Chadwick had been a fraud. I suppose I'd begun to think that the boy had come in for me *and* him, that it had been a sort of joint effort. But it struck me now that this is what Nelly had been about to say outside the Danish Kitchen – that it had all been down to me.

'But how *could* Chadwick be a fraud?'

Blundy poured more champagne.

'Saul Chadwick was the hot young medium of his day. John Morley was convinced he'd brought back the boy at a seance, so he established the trust in his favour. But Chadwick might have been motivated to cheat. That first trust guaranteed him a good lifestyle and income, but he was also eligible for certain...you might say performance-related monies from the philosophical society – from the second trust.'

'What's the full name of that organisation?' I cut in.

'Can't remember,' said Bundy. 'It's too long. They were – *are* – the intellectual overseers of the whole project, but maybe Chadwick and his assistants are too clever for them. Those tape recorders of his, for example. Are they recording sound or emitting it?' He drank champagne, before continuing, 'Then again he apparently seemed surprised by what turned up on that night in seventy-six, and he never matched it in any other session.'

Blundy was eyeing me. The bottle of champagne was empty. We'd motored *that* down all right.

'Fancy another?' said Blundy.

I nodded, and asked whether the séances were only ever held in The River House. He shook his head: 'Other locations associated with the kid as well. But always in York, of course.'

He raised his hand for the waitress. He began speaking about how the philosophical society could make a large amount of money available to any medium they considered able to contact the boy; how the surviving descendants of John Morley continued to be fascinated by Little Jack; how they might create another trust with a sole beneficiary; how they were in effect searching for the next Chadwick. As he did so, I shifted my focus from him to the window behind his back, and St Helen's Square beyond. It seems to me that the York citizenry behave better in the rain: they don't dawdle, shout or make mobile phone calls in the street. I saw two men going fast past the window wearing plain macs, and hats which I believed to be fedoras. One took something out of his inside pocket as he walked, and it was a long wallet, not a mobile phone.

The rain out there was floating down in a very friendly sort of way, illuminated by the blurred glow of the shops in the Square. It stood in very nicely for Christmas snow, and went well with 'Once In Royal David's City', which was now being cranked out by the man in fancy dress at the York Chimer. The second champagne had come and

Blundy was pouring, but I hardly noticed this because I was watching the wisps of smoke that were now floating through St Hélen's Square. Blundy was telling me something:

'There are certain facts known to very few people about Little Jack. People think they know but they don't. What did he like look like?'

The rain had increased somewhat, and I noticed that a boy had come up to the window of Betty's. He wore a raincoat with a wide belt around his middle; there may have been school books under his arm. He had dark hair that was combed straight back and held down by hair cream. His face was completely symmetrical, like a cat's or perhaps a bat's; he was very pale and his eyes were violet. He was inspecting the diners in Betty's Tea Rooms, scrutinising every person, searching for something.

'Well, I'll tell you this,' I heard myself saying to Blundy, 'He didn't look anything like the kid on the sweet tins. They were named after him, but he wasn't shown on them. His face would have frightened off the punters.'

I was distantly aware of Blundy, three feet in front of me, nodding his head, looking thoughtful and saying, in a new tone, 'You know, you're right, you're absolutely spot on. And why do you think he jumped? His father had a theory about this, but what do *you* think?'

The boy had finished his search; he was staring directly at me, and, as I spoke, he started to smile.

'He jumped in order to come back,' I said.

THE END